THE WAYFINDERS

Why Ancient Wisdom Matters in the Modern World

WADE DAVIS

This edition published in 2009 by
House of Anansi Press Inc.
110 Spadina Avenue, Suite 801
Toronto, ON, M5V 2K4
Tel. 416-363-4343
Fax 416-363-1017
www.anansi.ca

Distributed in Canada by
HarperCollins Canada Ltd.
1995 Markham Road
Scarborough, ON, M1B 5M8
Toll free tel. 1-800-387-0117

House of Anansi Press is committed to protecting our natural environment. As part of our efforts, this book is printed on paper that contains 100% post-consumer recycled fibres, is acid-free, and is processed chlorine-free.

13 12 11 10 09 1 2 3 4 5

LIBRARY AND ARCHIVES CANADA CATALOGUING IN PUBLICATION

Davis, Wade
The wayfinders : why ancient wisdom matters in the modern world / Wade Davis.

(CBC Massey lecture series)
ISBN 978-0-88784-842-1

1. Acculturation. 2. Language and culture. 3. Endangered languages.
4. Indigenous peoples—Languages. I. Title. II. Series: CBC Massey lecture series

GN366.W33 2009 303.48′2 C2009-903511-1

Cover design: Bill Douglas at The Bang
Text design: Ingrid Paulson
Typesetting: Sari Naworynski

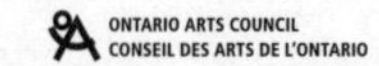

We acknowledge for their financial support of our publishing program the Canada Council for the Arts, the Ontario Arts Council, and the Government of Canada through the Book Publishing Industry Development Program (BPIDP).

Printed and bound in Canada

For David Maybury-Lewis
1929–2007

THE WAYFINDERS

ONE

SEASON OF THE BROWN HYENA

"I want all the cultures of all lands to be blown about my house as freely as possible. But I refuse to be blown off my feet by any." — Mahatma Gandhi

ONE OF THE INTENSE pleasures of travel is the opportunity to live amongst peoples who have not forgotten the old ways, who still feel their past in the wind, touch it in stones polished by rain, taste it in the bitter leaves of plants. Just to know that, in the Amazon, Jaguar shaman still journey beyond the Milky Way, that the myths of the Inuit elders still resonate with meaning, that the Buddhists in Tibet still pursue the breath of the Dharma is to remember the central revelation of anthropology: the idea that the social world in which we live does not exist in some absolute sense, but rather is simply one model of reality, the consequence of one set of intellectual and spiritual choices that our particular cultural lineage made, however successfully, many generations ago.

But whether we travel with the nomadic Penan in the forests of Borneo, a Vodoun acolyte in Haiti, a *curandero* in the high Andes of Peru, a Tamashek *caravanseri* in the red sands of the Sahara, or a yak herder on the slopes of Chomolungma, all these peoples teach us that there are other options, other possibilities, other ways of thinking and interacting with the earth. This is an idea that can only fill us with hope.

Together the myriad of cultures makes up an intellectual and spiritual web of life that envelops the planet and is every bit as important to the well being of the planet as is the biological web of life that we know as the biosphere. You might think of this social web of life as an *"ethnosphere,"* a term perhaps best defined as the sum total of all thoughts and intuitions, myths and beliefs, ideas and inspirations brought into being by the human imagination since the dawn of consciousness. The ethnosphere is humanity's greatest legacy. It is the product of our dreams, the embodiment of our hopes, the symbol of all we are and all that we, as a wildly inquisitive and astonishingly adaptive species, have created.

And just as the biosphere, the biological matrix of life, is being severely eroded by the destruction of habitat and the resultant loss of plant and animal species, so too is the ethnosphere, only at a far greater rate. No biologist, for example, would suggest that 50 percent of all species are moribund. Yet this, the most apocalyptic scenario in the realm of biological diversity, scarcely approaches what we know to be the most optimistic scenario in the realm of cultural diversity.

The key indicator, the canary in the coal mine if you will, is language loss. A language, of course, is not merely a set of grammatical rules or a vocabulary. It is a flash of the human spirit, the vehicle by which the soul of each particular culture comes into the material world. Every language is an old-growth forest of the mind, a watershed of thought, an ecosystem of spiritual possibilities.

Of the 7,000 languages spoken today, fully half are not being taught to children. Effectively, unless something changes, they will disappear within our lifetimes. Half of the languages of the world are teetering on the brink of extinction. Just think about it. What could be more lonely than to be enveloped in silence, to be the last of your people to speak your native tongue, to have no way to pass on the wisdom of your ancestors or anticipate the promise of your descendants. This tragic fate is indeed the plight of someone somewhere on earth roughly every two weeks. On average, every fortnight an elder dies and carries with him or her into the grave the last syllables of an ancient tongue. What this really means is that within a generation or two, we will be witnessing the loss of fully half of humanity's social, cultural and intellectual legacy. This is the hidden backdrop of our age.

There are those who quite innocently ask, "Wouldn't the world be a better place if we all spoke the same language? Would not communication be facilitated, making it easier for us to get along?" My answer is always to say, "A wonderful idea, but let's make that universal language Haida or Yoruba, Lakota, Inuktitut or San." Suddenly people get a sense of what it would mean to be unable to speak their mother tongue. I cannot imagine a world in which I could not speak English, for not only is it a beautiful language, it's my language, the full expression of who I am. But at the same time I don't want it to sweep away the other voices of humanity, the other languages of the world, like some kind of cultural nerve gas.

Languages, of course, have come and gone through history. Babylonian is no longer spoken in the streets of Baghdad, or Latin in the hills of Italy. But again the biological analogy is useful. Extinction is a natural phenomenon, but in general, speciation, the evolution of new forms of life, has outpaced loss over the last 600 million years, making the world an ever more diverse place. When the sounds of Latin faded from Rome, they found new expression in the Romance languages. Today, just as plants and animals are disappearing in what biologists recognize as an unprecedented wave of extinction, so too languages are dying at such a rate that they leave in their wake no descendants.

While biologists suggest that perhaps 20 percent of mammals, 11 percent of birds, and 5 percent of fish are threatened, and botanists anticipate the loss of 10 percent of floristic diversity, linguists and anthropologists today bear witness to the imminent disappearance of half the extant languages of the world. Over six hundred have fewer than a hundred speakers. Some 3,500 are kept alive by a fifth of 1 percent of the global population. The ten most prevalent languages, by contrast, are thriving; they are the mother tongues of half of humanity. Fully 80 percent of the world's population communicates with one of just eighty-three languages. But what of the poetry, songs, and knowledge encoded in the other voices, those cultures that are the guardians and custodians of 98.8 percent of the world's linguistic diversity? Is the wisdom of an elder any less important simply because he or she communicates to an audience of one? Is the value of a people a simple correlate of their numbers? To the contrary, every culture is by definition a vital branch of our family tree, a repository of knowledge and experience, and, if given the opportunity, a source of inspiration and promise for the future. "When you lose a language," the MIT linguist Ken Hale remarked not long before he passed away, "you lose a culture, intellectual wealth, a work of art. It's like dropping a bomb on the Louvre."

But what exactly is at stake? What, if anything, should be done about it? A number of books over recent years have paid homage to the global sweep of technology and modernity, suggesting that the world is flat, that one does not have to emigrate to innovate, that we are fusing into a single reality, dominated by a specific model of economics, that the future is to be found everywhere and all at once. When I read these books I can only think that I must have been travelling in very different circles than these writers. The world that I have been fortunate to know, as I hope these lectures will demonstrate, is most assuredly *not* flat. It is full of peaks and valleys, curious anomalies and divine distractions. History has not stopped, and the processes of cultural change and transformation remain as dynamic today as ever. The world can only appear monochromatic to those who persist in interpreting what they experience through the lens of a single cultural paradigm, their own. For those with the eyes to see and the heart to feel, it remains a rich and complex topography of the spirit.

IT MAY SEEM UNUSUAL to begin a celebration of culture and diversity with a nod to genetics, but this is really where the story begins. For nearly ten years my friend and colleague at the National Geographic Society, Spencer Wells, has been leading the Genographic Project, an ambitious global effort to track through both space and time the primordial journey of humanity. What he and other population geneticists have discovered is one of the great revelations of modern science. We are, as Spencer reminds us, the result of over a billion years of evolutionary transformations. Our DNA, encoded in four simple letters, is a historical document that reaches back to the origin of life. Each one of us is a chapter in the greatest story ever written, a narrative of exploration and discovery remembered not only in myth but encoded in our blood.

Every cell in our bodies is charged by a miracle, a double helix of four molecule types, four simple letters, A, C, G and T, linked in complex sequences that help orchestrate every pulse of sentient existence. There are six billion bits of data wrapped and coiled and spun in the darkness of our beings. If the DNA in any human body were to be stretched out in a single line it would reach not just to the moon, but to 3,000 celestial spheres equidistant from the earth. In life, of course, this chain, this mystic inheritance, is broken and bundled into forty-six chromosomes, which pass down through the generations. With each new coupling, each new child, these chromosomes are shuffled and reassembled such that each of us is born as a unique combination of the genetic endowment of our parents.

But vital clues remain. In each cell's nucleus, the Y chromosome, the factor that determines male gender, a sweep of some 50 million nucleotides, passes more or less intact through the generations, from father to son. In each cell's mitochondria, its energy-producing organelles, the DNA also passes more or less intact through the generations, but from mother to daughter. Because of this, and only because of this, these two threads of DNA act as a sort of time machine, opening a window onto the past.

Almost all human DNA, 99.9 percent of the three billion nucleotides, does not vary from person to person. But woven into the remaining 0.1 percent are revelations, differences in the raw code itself that yield vital clues about human ancestry. Inevitably during the transcription and replication of genetic information, these billions of bits of data, small glitches occur. Where the letter A ought to be, there appears a G. These are mutations, and they happen all the time. They are not cataclysmic. Rarely would a single mutation make for phenotypic changes. A shift in a single letter of the code does not change the colour of the skin, the height of the body, let alone the intelligence and destiny of the person. This genetic drift does, however, remain indelibly encoded in the genes of that individual's descendants. These single inherited mutations are the markers, the "seams and spot welds," as Spencer has written, that over the last twenty years have allowed population geneticists to reconstruct the story of human origins and migration with a precision that would have been unimaginable a generation ago. By studying not the similarities but the differences in the DNA between individuals, by tracking the appearance of markers through time, and by looking at thousands of markers, the lineages of descent can be determined. Two entwined evolutionary trees are being constructed, one through fathers and sons, the other through mothers and daughters, and the entire journey of humanity both in time and space brought into remarkably precise focus.

The overwhelming scientific consensus suggests that all of humanity lived in Africa until some 60,000 years ago. Then, perhaps driven by changing climatic and ecological conditions that led to the desertification of the African grasslands, a small band of men, women, and children, possibly as few as 150 individuals, walked out of the ancient continent and began the colonization of the world. What propelled the multiple waves of the human diaspora can never be fully known, though presumably food and other resource imperatives played a major role. As populations grew beyond the carrying capacity of the land, they splintered, and some bands moved on. What the DNA record reveals is that as smaller groups split off, they carried only a subset of the genetic diversity originally present in the African population. Indeed, the science indicates that for all human cultures, wherever they ended up, genetic diversity decreases the further both in time and space that a people are removed from Africa. Again, these differences do not reflect phenotype. They do not imply anything about human potential. They are simply markers that highlight a sort of cosmic map of culture, revealing where and when our ancestors took to the open road.

A first wave followed the shoreline of Asia, traversing the underbelly of Asia to reach Australia by as early as 50,000 BP. A second migration moved north through the Middle East and then turned east, dividing once again some 40,000 years ago, sending movements south into India, west and south through Southeast Asia to southern China, and north into Central Asia. From here, out of the brooding mountains at the heart of the world's largest continent, two subsequent migrations brought people west to Europe (30,000 BP) and east to Siberia, which was populated by 20,000 BP. Finally, some 12,000 years ago, even as a new wave came out of the Middle East into southeastern Europe, and people moved north through China, a small band of hunters crossed the land bridge of Beringia and established for the first time a human presence in the Americas. Within 2,000 years their descendants had reached Tierra del Fuego. From humble origins in Africa, after a journey that lasted 2,500 generations, a hegira 40,000 years in the making, our species had settled the entire habitable world.

BEFORE GOING ANY FURTHER, let me explain why I think this genetic research is so important, for this really provides the foundation for all of the themes and issues that will be discussed in these lectures. Nothing that has emerged from science in my lifetime, save perhaps the vision of the Earth from space brought home by Apollo, has done more to liberate the human spirit from the parochial tyrannies that have haunted us since the birth of memory.

As a social anthropologist I was trained to believe in the primacy of history and culture as the key determinants in human affairs. Nurture, if you will, as opposed to nature. Anthropology began as an attempt to decipher the exotic other, with the hope that by embracing the wonder of distinct and novel cultural possibilities, we might enrich our appreciation and understanding of human nature and our own humanity. Very early on, however, the discipline was hijacked by the ideology of its times. As naturalists throughout the nineteenth century attempted to classify creation even as they coped with the revelations of Darwin, anthropologists became servants of the Crown, agents dispatched to the far reaches of empire with the task of understanding strange tribal peoples and cultures that they might properly be administered and controlled.

Evolutionary theory, distilled from the study of bird beaks, beetles, and barnacles, slipped into social theory in a manner that proved useful to the age. It was anthropologist Herbert Spencer who coined the phrase "survival of the fittest." At a time when the United States was being built by the labour of African slaves, and the British class system was so stratified that children of the wealthy were on average 6 inches taller than those of the poor, a theory that provided a scientific rationale for differences in race and class was a welcome convenience.

Evolution suggested change through time, and this, together with the Victorian cult of improvement, implied a progression in the affairs of human beings, a ladder to success that rose from the primitive to the civilized, from the tribal village of Africa to London and the splendour of the Strand. The cultures of the world came to be seen as a living museum in which individual societies represented evolutionary moments captured and mired in time, each one a stage in the imagined ascent to civilization. It followed with the certainty of Victorian rectitude that advanced societies had an obligation to assist the backward, to civilize the savage, a moral duty that again played well into the needs of empire. "We happen to be the best people in the world," Cecil Rhodes famously said, "and the more of the world we inhabit, the better it is for humanity." George Nathaniel Curzon, eleventh viceroy of India, agreed. "There has never been anything," he wrote, "so great in the world's history as the British Empire, so great an instrument for the good of humanity. We must devote all of our energies and our lives to maintaining it." Asked why there was not a single Indian native employed in the Government of India, he replied, "Because among all 300 million people of the subcontinent, there was not a single man capable of the job."

Having established the primacy of race, and the inherent superiority of Victorian England, anthropologists set out to prove their case. The scientific mismeasure of man began as phrenologists with calipers and rulers detected and recorded minute differences in skull morphology, which were presumed to reflect innate differences in intelligence. Before long, physical anthropologists were measuring and photographing peoples throughout the world, all with the deeply flawed notion that a complete classification of our species could be attained simply by comparing body parts, the shape of hips, the texture of hair, and inevitably the colour of skin. Linnaeus, the father of classification, had in the late eighteenth century determined that all humans belonged to the same species, *Homo sapiens*, "man the wise." But he hedged his bets by distinguishing five subspecies, which he identified as *afer* (African), *americanus* (Native American), *asiaticus* (Asian), *europaeus* (European) and finally a catch-all taxon, *monstrosus*, which included essentially everybody else, all the peoples so bizarre to the European eye that they defied classification.

More than a century after Linnaeus, physical anthropology, inspired by a selective misreading of Darwin, accepted the concept of race as a given. The confirmation of such preconceptions became part of the agenda and duty of both scholars and explorers. Among those who set out to chart the racial saga was a British army officer and explorer, Thomas Whiffen. Travelling down the Río Putumayo in the Colombian Amazon at the height of the rubber terror, he described the forest as "innately malevolent, a horrible, most evil-disposed enemy. The air is heavy with the fumes of fallen vegetation slowly steaming to decay. The gentle Indian, peaceful and loving, is a fiction of perfervid imaginations only. The Indians are innately cruel." Living for a year among them, Whiffen noted, was to become "nauseated by their bestiality." At a time when literally thousands of Bora and Huitoto Indians were being enslaved and slaughtered, he offered advice to future travellers, suggesting that exploratory parties be limited to no more than twenty-five individuals. "On this principle," he wrote, "it will be seen that the smaller the quantity of baggage carried, the greater will be the number of rifles available for the security of the expedition."

Whiffen, whose book, *The North-West Amazons*, was widely read when published in 1915, claimed to have come upon cannibal feasts, "prisoners eaten to the last bit, a mad festival of savagery ... men whose eyes glare, nostrils quiver ... an all pervading delirium." Other academic explorers of the era, if somewhat more restrained, nevertheless subscribed to what Michael Taussig has charitably called the "penis school of physical anthropology." The French anthropologist Eugenio Robuchon, who also descended the Putumayo, the River of Death, noted that, "in general the Huitotos have thin and nervous members." Another chapter of his book begins: "The Huitoto have gray-copper skin whose tones correspond to numbers 29 and 30 of the chromatic scale of the Anthropological Society of Paris." A footnote in Whiffen's book reads, "Robuchon states that the women's mammae are pyriform, and the photographs show distinctly pyriform breasts with digitiform nipples. I found them resembling rather the segment of a sphere, the areola not prominent, and the nipples hemispherical."

Not everyone was interested in the measurement of breasts and skulls. Those who preferred to look forward to a brighter world distorted Darwinian theory in anticipation of creating a new and better society. Eugenics means "good birth," and the movement that flourished at the turn of the twentieth century called for the selective breeding of healthy and fit individuals, with the goal of improving the gene pool of humanity. By the 1920s this ideal had been inverted into a rationale for forced sterilization and the culling of deviance. If one could improve the gene pool through selective breeding, surely one could achieve the same goal by eliminating from the stock elements deemed to be undesirable. This was the twisted scientific principle that in time allowed the Germans to justify the slaughter and systematic extermination of millions of innocent people.

Given this sordid history, the ludicrous ambitions of phrenology, the murderous consequences of eugenics, the perennial confidence and hubris of the scientific community even when promoting the most dubious of claims, it is no wonder that many people, notably those from non-Western traditions, remain deeply skeptical of any sweeping theory of human origins and migration. That such research is dependent on the collection and analysis of human blood from remote and isolated populations only further inflames passions and concerns. Indigenous peoples, in particular, are deeply offended by the suggestion that their homelands, enshrined in narrative and myth, may not have been inhabited by their ancestors since the dawn of time. There have even been accusations that the recent scientific revelations about our genetic heritage may prompt open conflict and the forced removal of tribal peoples from lands that they have in fact occupied for all living memory.

I am quite certain that these fears are unfounded. History suggests that dominant groups do not need excuses to ravage the weak, and I do not believe that any theory that emerges from these new studies will somehow tip the balance and in and of itself lead to the disenfranchisement of a people. It is true that the Nazis turned to pseudoscience about genetics and race to rationalize genocide, but, as Steven Pinker reminds us, the Marxist–Leninists were inspired to equally despicable and devastating acts of genocide by their pseudoscientific fantasies about the social malleability of human nature. "The real threat to humanity," Pinker writes, "comes from totalizing ideologies and the denial of human rights, rather than curiosity about nature and nurture."

Knowledge poses no threat to culture. What's more, these research efforts only generate a certain type of knowledge, defined within a specific world view. Western science by definition rejects a literal interpretation of origin myths that root the Haida, for example, to Haida Gwaii. But that rejection does nothing to quell the spirit of the Haida or to persuade my friend Guujaaw, head of the Council for the Haida Nation, that his people have not occupied the archipelago since human beings emerged from the clamshell and Raven slipped out of the ether to steal the sun. A scientific suggestion that the Haida may have "come from somewhere else" has already been made; it has long been the foundation of orthodox anthropology. But this scientific "truth" does nothing to limit the authority and power of the Haida today. Their ability to deal nation to nation with the Canadian government has little to do with mythic ancestral claims and everything to do with political power, a priori evidence of occupancy at the time of contact, and the ability of leaders such as Guujaaw to mobilize support for his people throughout the world.

Science is only one way of knowing, and its purpose is not to generate absolute truths but rather to inspire better and better ways of thinking about phenomena. As recently as 1965, American anthropologist Carleton Coon wrote two books, *The Origin of Races* and *The Living Races of Man,* in which he advanced the theory that there were five distinct human subspecies. Little, apparently, had been learned since the time of Linnaeus. The political and technological dominance of Europeans, Coon suggested, was a natural consequence of their evolved genetic superiority. He even asserted that "racial intermixture can upset the genetic as well as the social equilibrium of a group." Coon at the time was the president of the American Association of Physical Anthropologists, a full professor at the University of Pennsylvania, and curator of ethnology at the university's Museum of Archaeology and Anthropology.

That such statements, convenient as they were during the last years of Jim Crow and segregation, were seriously entertained by the academic community as recently as 1965 should certainly give us pause as we consider the implications of the new research in population genetics. But when the science in fact suggests an end to race, when it reveals beyond any reasonable doubt that race is a fiction, it behooves us to listen. We should at least hope that for once the scientists have it right.

And they do. They have revealed beyond any doubt that the genetic endowment of humanity is a single continuum. From Ireland to Japan, from the Amazon to Siberia, there are no sharp genetic differences among populations. There are only geographical gradients. The most remote society on earth contains within its people fully 85 percent of our total genetic diversity. Were the rest of humanity to be swept away by plague or war, the Waorani or the Barasana, the Rendille or the Tuareg would have within their blood the genetic endowment of all of humanity. Like a sacred repository of spirit and mind, any one of these cultures, any one of the 7,000, could provide the seeds from which humanity in all its diversity might be reborn.

What all of this means is that biologists and population geneticists have at last proved to be true something that philosophers have always dreamed: We are all literally brothers and sisters. We are all cut from the same genetic cloth.

It follows, by definition, that all cultures share essentially the same mental acuity, the same raw genius. Whether this intellectual capacity and potential is exercised in stunning works of technological innovation, as has been the great achievement of the West, or through the untangling of the complex threads of memory inherent in a myth — a primary concern, for example, of the Aborigines of Australia — is simply a matter of choice and orientation, adaptive insights and cultural priorities.

There is no hierarchy of progress in the history of culture, no Social Darwinian ladder to success. The Victorian notion of the savage and the civilized, with European industrial society sitting proudly at the apex of a pyramid of advancement that widens at the base to the so-called primitives of the world, has been thoroughly discredited — indeed, scientifically ridiculed for the racial and colonial conceit that it was. The brilliance of scientific research and the revelations of modern genetics have affirmed in an astonishing way the essential connectedness of humanity. We share a sacred endowment, a common history written in our bones. It follows, as these lectures will suggest, that the myriad of cultures of the world are not failed attempts at modernity, let alone failed attempts to be us. They are unique expressions of the human imagination and heart, unique answers to a fundamental question: What does it mean to be human and alive? When asked this question, the cultures of the world respond in 7,000 different voices, and these collectively comprise our human repertoire for dealing with all the challenges that will confront us as a species over the next 2,500 generations, even as we continue this never-ending journey.

BUT WHO WERE THESE people who walked out of Africa so many thousands of years ago? What were they like? If we can track their subsequent journey through inherited genetic markers, presumably it should be possible to find a people still living in Africa, a people who never left, and whose DNA therefore lacks all evidence of the mutations that occurred among the successive waves that spread our ancestors throughout the world. As Spencer Wells' research again highlights, such a people have indeed been identified, and they are a culture that has fascinated anthropologists for decades. Living today in the searing sands of the

Kalahari, 55,000 strong scattered across some 84,000 square kilometres of Botswana, Namibia and southern Angola, the San have long been considered the descendants of a people who at one time inhabited the entire subcontinent and much of East Africa. Displaced by successive waves of agriculturalists and pastoral herders, the San survived as bushmen, nomadic hunters and gatherers, men and women whose precise and exacting knowledge allowed their people alone to survive in one of the most forbidding and parsimonious desert landscapes on earth. This extraordinary body of adaptive information, this intellectual toolbox, is encoded in the words and sounds of a native tongue that is a linguistic marvel, a language totally unrelated to any other known family of languages. In everyday English we use 31 sounds. The language of the San has 141, a cacophony of cadence and clicks that many linguists believe echoes the very birth of language. Indeed, the genetic data suggests that this may be the case. The absence of key markers indicates that the San were the first people in what became the family tree of humanity. If the Irish and the Lakota, the Hawaiian and the Maya are the branches and limbs, the San are the trunk, and quite possibly the oldest culture in the world. When the rest of us decided to travel, the San elected to stay home.

Certainly until the early years of the twentieth century, when the impact of alcohol and education, and the false and twisted promises of development, shattered many of their lives, the San had followed the rhythm of their natural world for perhaps 10,000 years. They had little choice. Their very survival depended on their ability to anticipate every nuance of the seasons, every movement of the animals, the very sounds that plants make as they grow. Water was the constant challenge. In the Kalahari there is no standing water for ten months of the year. Water has to be found in the hollows of trees, sucked from beneath the mud with hollow reeds, or cached in ostrich eggs, plugged with grass and marked with a sign of the owner. For most of the year the only source of water is liquid found in roots or squeezed from the guts of animals.

During the dry season, May through the end of December, the San are constantly on the move. Though they think of themselves primarily as hunters, they survive by eating plants, with each adult consuming 5 kilograms of wild melon a day. When the melons wither, the San find they must dig, and in a desert environment where the body loses 3 litres a day in sweat, it takes more than twenty large tubers, each dug from the sand, to keep a person alive. In the worst months, the Season of the Brown Hyena, the San scrape hollows in the ground, moisten the earth with urine, and then lie completely still beneath a sprinkling of sand, tormented by flies, as they wait out the heat of the day. The sun is not a source of life, but a symbol of death. The time of greatest privation is also the time of promise, for in October begin the Little Rains, the first teasing raindrops heralding the end of the period of drought. For three months, from October through December, the land is tormented by this promise of rain, which is never enough. Those fortunate to live around permanent water huddle in small encampments. The majority forage by dusk and dawn for roots. The heat continues and dry winds sweep over the brown grasslands, and the spirits of the dead appear as dust devils spinning across a grey and yellow horizon.

Finally, in January arrive the rains and for three months the people celebrate a season of rebirth and regeneration. But in the Kalahari, rain remains relative. Sometimes the clouds swell into massive thunderheads, and crack open the sky to pound the earth with 8 centimetres of rain in an hour. But there are years when the rains simply do not arrive, and precipitation for the entire wet season is as little as 5 centimetres. The people must dig as deep as several metres beneath the surface of the earth to reach an impervious layer where water may sometimes be found. The possibility of dying of thirst is a constant, even in the season of the rains.

In good years the rains bring relative abundance. Pools of water form on the sand, and equipped only with digging sticks, collecting bags, woven nets and ostrich shells to carry water, the people move about in small bands, extended family units that occasionally come together in larger concentrations to celebrate a harvest of fruits or seeds, the presence of game. These wanderings are not random. Each passage traverses known ground, time-honoured territories that resonate with narratives, each granting ownership of a particular resource to a band of people — a resource that might be a tree or shrub, or a recognized source of honey, the most highly prized of nectars. The Mother of the Bees is the wife of the Great God who created all things. A fount of honey is protected by name, and to violate another's claim is a crime punishable by death.

The favourite time of year is the month of April, the Season of the Hunter. Though plants comprise the bulk of the San diet, meat is the most desired food, as it is the hunt that transforms a boy into a man. By April in most years, the rains have driven away the heat, and the bitter cold of desert winter has yet to set in. There is ripe food everywhere — beneath the ground, upon the vines, on every limb of every tree and shrub. The antelope, having calved their young, are fat and plentiful. Territory is forgotten as the men range across the desert in small hunting parties, walking as far as 60 kilometres in a day, returning to the fire and the families each night. They travel light: short bow and a quiver of arrows made from root bark capped in the scrotum of the prey; fire-making sticks; a hollow reed for sucking water; a knife and short spear; a blob of vegetable gum to make repairs; a sharpened stick for holding meat to flame.

Hunting in teams, the San men watch for signs. Nothing escapes their notice: a bend in a blade of grass, the direction of the tug that snapped a twig, the depth, shape, and condition of a track. Everything is written in the sand. Adultery among the San is a challenge because every human footprint is recognizable. From a single animal track, San hunters can discern direction, time, and rate of travel. Armed with ingenuity, and living in direct competition with serious predators such as leopards and lions, they manage to kill an astonishing array of creatures. With pits of poisoned stakes they lay traps for hippos. Risking their lives, they run upon the heels of elephants, hamstringing the enormous animals with the swift blow of an axe. Hovering near a lion kill, they wait until the animal is satiated, and then chase the sluggish cat from the carcass of the dead. Birds are snared on the fly with nets. Antelope are literally run to ground, often over a period of days. The San bows are short, with little power and an effective range of perhaps 25 metres. The arrows rarely penetrate the prey. They nick the skin, but generally this is enough, for the arrows are tipped in deadly toxin derived from the grubs of two species of beetles that feed on the leaves of a desert tree, *Commiphora africana*. The San find the beetles in colonies and excavate the cocoons, which they store in containers made from antelope horn. They roll the grubs back and forth between the fingers, softening the insides without breaking the skin. These they squeeze to exude a paste. Sun-dried, the venom, once injected into the blood, provokes convulsions, paralysis, and death.

The hunt is the metaphor that brings us into the very heart of San life. A man who does not hunt remains a child. To marry, a man must bring meat to the parents of the bride. A first antelope kill is the high point of youth, a moment recorded for all time in the skin of the hunter by his father, who makes a shallow incision with bone, and rubs into the wound a compound of meat and fat, scarring the right side of the body if the kill is a buck, the left if a doe. The tattoo marks the boy with the heart of a hunter — a potent source of magic, for the San do not simply kill game. They engage in a dance with the prey, a ritual exchange that ends with the creature literally making of itself an offering, a sacrifice. Every hunt ends in exhaustion, as the antelope realizes that whatever it does it cannot escape the pursuit of man. It then stops and turns, and the arrow flies.

The meat of large prey is shared among all members of an encampment, the distribution determined not by the hunter but by the owner of the arrow. San men are always giving each other gifts of arrows. The arrow, with its tip of bone, its elegant shaft, its perfect blend of poison, represents the highest achievement of San technology. But its power lies in the realm of the social, for each exchange of arrows establishes bonds of reciprocity that forge the solidarity of San lives. To refuse a gift is an act of hostility. To accept is to acknowledge both a connection and an obligation. The arrow represents much more than a debt that must be honoured by trade, or reimbursed over time. Rather, it secures a lifelong duty that welds the individual to the greater social sphere, brings the youth into the realm of the hunter, and the hunter into the circle of the hearth and the sacred fire.

If the San associate the sun with death, fire symbolizes life, the unity of the people, the survival of the family. Whereas a gift of meat formalizes the betrothal of a woman, divorce is finalized the moment she simply returns to her family's fire. A mother gives birth in the darkness, and announces the delivery by moving back into the circle of firelight. When an elder grows too old and weak to continue with the people, he is left behind to die, protected from the hyenas by a circle of thorn scrub and a fire at his feet to light his way into the next world. For the San there are two great spirits: the Great God of the Eastern Sky; and the lesser God of the West, a source of negativity and darkness, the custodian of the dead. To ward off the God of the West, to deflect the arrows of disease and misfortune, the San dance around the fire, casting their beings into trance. The vital force of life that resides in the belly rises up the spine as a vapour, touches the base of the skull, diffuses through the body, and spins the spirit into a higher consciousness. The healing dance ends with the hunters around the fire, having teased the flames and the gods by placing their own heads in the burning coals.

LANGUAGE, STEALTH, SPIRIT, adaptive genius — these were the tools that allowed the San to survive the Kalahari. And these too presumably were the attributes that our distant ancestors carried out of Africa. But an ethnographic portrait of the San today, or the San as they lived before the ravages of modern colonialism, still leaves us with fundamental questions: How can we reach back in time to touch the essence of these earth wanderers, these ancestral beings who found their way to every habitable place on the planet? What did they know? How did they think? What inspired them, beyond the raw challenges of staying alive? What ignited, as my good friend the poet Clayton Eshleman has so beautifully inquired, the "juniper fuse" of the imagination, for surely this must have marked the true moment of human origins, the unfolding of consciousness that led to the creation of culture. At some point it all began.

We know that the hominid lineage dates back in Africa for millions of years: the earliest skeletal remains are those of a three-year-old girl discovered in 2006 in the Afar Desert of Ethiopia by paleoanthropologist Zeresenay Alemseged. He named her *Australopithecus afarensis,* after the place where she was found and where her bones had rested for 3.3 million years. Our own species, *Homo sapiens,* did not evolve until a mere 200,000 years ago. We had direct competitors. The human population ebbed and flowed, and at one juncture we were very nearly extinguished, reduced perhaps to a thousand individuals. But something pulled us back from extinction.

For most of our history we shared the world with another branch on the hominid tree, our remote cousins the Neanderthals, who were descendants of the same progenitor, *Homo erectus*. Neanderthals clearly had awareness. They used tools, and there is evidence of deliberate burial as early as 70,000 years ago. But whether it was an increase in the size of the brain, the development of language, or some other evolutionary catalyst, our species possessed competitive advantages that ultimately would launch its destiny in an astonishing manner, an explosion of intellect that left Neanderthal man gasping for survival.

The place to witness this primordial flash of the spirit lies beneath the ground in southwest France and beyond the Pyrenees in Spain. By the time the last vestiges of Neanderthal life slipped away from Europe 27,000 years ago, the stunning Upper Paleolithic cave art, created by our direct ancestors, was already several thousand years old. Reaching deep into the earth, through narrow passages that opened into chambers illuminated by the flicker of tallow lamps, men and women drew with stark realism the animals they revered, singly or in herds, using the contour of the stone to animate forms so dramatically that entire caverns come alive even today with creatures long since lost to extinction.

The sophistication of the figurative art found at Chauvet and Altamira, and at later sites such as Lascaux and Pech Merle, is astonishing not only for its transcendent beauty, but also for what it tells us about the fluorescence of human potential once brought into being by culture. The technical skills, the exploitation of red ochre and black manganese, iron oxide and charcoal, to yield a full palette of colours, the use of scaffolding, the diverse techniques to apply the pigments, are themselves remarkable and suggest a relatively high level of social organization and specialization that is echoed in the genius of the Upper Paleolithic tool kit, the elegant scrapers and blades pounded from flint. The use of negative space and shadow, the sense of composition and perspective, the superimposition of animal forms through time indicates a highly evolved artistic aesthetic that itself implies the expression of some deeper yearning.

I recently spent a month in France in the Dordogne with Clayton Eshleman, who has been studying the cave art for more than thirty years, ever since a fateful morning in the spring of 1974 when he abandoned, as he put it, the world of bird song and blue sky for a realm of constricted darkness that filled his being with "mystical enthusiasm." Like so many observers before him he was dazzled yet perplexed not just by what he saw but how he felt in the sensory isolation of the caves, his imagination suspended between consciousness and the soul of an all-devouring earth, a "living and fathomless reservoir of psychic force." He paid attention not only to what was depicted on the rock, but also to what was missing — the bison and the horse being the most commonly portrayed animals, with carnivores represented the least. The images float in isolation; there are no backgrounds or ground lines. Depictions of people are few, and there are no displays of fighting, no scenes of hunting, no representation of physical conflict.

Northrop Frye struggled in vain to assign purpose to these works. "We can add such words as *religion* and *magic*," he wrote, "but the fact remains that the complexity, urgency and sheer titanic power of the motivation involved is something we cannot understand now, much less recapture." Frye saw the animals portrayed as a "kind of extension of human consciousness and power into the objects of greatest energy and strength they [the humans] could see in the world around them." It was as if in painting these forms onto rock, the artist was somehow assimilating the "energy, the beauty, the elusive glory latent in nature to the observing mind." We look at the animal forms with human eyes and "suspect that we are really seeing a sorcerer or shaman who has identified himself with the animal by putting on its skin."

Clayton, too, sensed that the cave art did much more than invoke the magic of the hunt. Human beings, he suggested, were at one time of an animal nature, and then at some point, whether we want to admit it or not, were not. The art pays homage to that moment when human beings, through consciousness, separated themselves from the animal realm, emerging as the unique entity that we now know ourselves to be. Viewed in this light the art may be seen — as Clayton has written — almost as "postcards of nostalgia," laments for a lost time when animals and people were as one. Proto-shamanism, the first great spiritual impulse, grew as an attempt to reconcile and even re-establish through ritual a separation that was irrevocable. What is perhaps most remarkable is the fact that the fundamentals of Upper Paleolithic art remained essentially unchanged for literally 20,000 years, five times the chronological distance that separates us today from the builders of the Great Pyramid at Giza. If these were postcards of nostalgia, ours was a very long farewell indeed.

The cave art marked also the beginning of our discontent, the restless quest for meaning and understanding that has propelled the human dream ever since. Our entire existential experience as a species over the past 50,000 years may be distilled into two words: *how* and *why*. These are the departure points for all inquiry, the slivers of insight around which cultures have crystallized.

All peoples face the same adaptive imperatives. We all must give birth; raise, educate and protect our children; console our elders as they move into their final years. Virtually all cultures would endorse most tenets of the Ten Commandments, not because the Judaic world was uniquely inspired, but because it articulated the rules that allowed a social species to thrive. Few societies fail to outlaw murder or thievery. All create traditions that bring consistency to coupling and procreation. Every culture honours its dead, even as it struggles with the meaning of the inexorable separation that death implies.

Given these common challenges, the range and diversity of cultural adaptations is astonishing. Hunting and gathering societies have flourished from the rain forests of Southeast Asia and the Amazon to the dry flat deserts of Australia; from the Kalahari to the remote, icy reaches of the high Arctic; from the broad American plains to the pampas of Patagonia. Wayfarers and fishermen have settled virtually every island chain in all the world's oceans. Complex societies have been built on the bounty of the sea alone, the salmon, eulachon, and herring that brought life to the First Nations of the Pacific Northwest.

With the Neolithic revolution some 10,000 years ago, humans began to domesticate plants and animals. Pastoral nomads settled the marginal reaches of the planet: the sands of the Sahara, the Tibetan plateau, and the windswept expanses of the Asian steppe. Agriculturalists took a handful of grasses — wheat, barley, rice, oats, millet and maize — and from their bounty generated surpluses, food that could be stored, thus allowing for hierarchy, specialization, and sedentary life: all the hallmarks of civilization, as traditionally defined. Great cities arose, and, in time, kingdoms, empires, and nation-states.

No series of lectures can do justice to the full wonder of the human cultural experience. The very word *culture* defies precise definition, even as the concept embraces multitudes. A small, isolated society of a few hundred men and women in the mountains of New Guinea has its own culture, but so, too, do countries such as Ireland and France. Distinct cultures may share similar spiritual beliefs — indeed, this is the norm in lands that have been inspired by Christianity, Islam, and Buddhism. While language in general tends to delineate unique world views, there are peoples in Alaska, for example, that have lost the ability to speak in their native tongues, yet still maintain a thriving and vibrant sense of culture.

Perhaps the closest we can come to a meaningful definition of *culture* is the acknowledgement that each is a unique and ever-changing constellation we recognize through the observation and study of its language, religion, social and economic organization, decorative arts, stories, myths, ritual practices and beliefs, and a host of other adaptive traits and characteristics. The full measure of a culture embraces both the actions of a people and the quality of their aspirations, the nature of the metaphors that propel their lives. And no description of a people can be complete without reference to the character of their homeland, the ecological and geographical matrix in which they have determined to live out their destiny. Just as landscape defines character, culture springs from a spirit of place.

Over the course of these lectures I look forward to exploring some of these worlds with you. We'll travel to Polynesia and celebrate the art of navigation that allowed the wayfinders to infuse the entire Pacific Ocean with their imagination and genius. In the Amazon await the descendants of a true lost civilization, the Peoples of the Anaconda, a complex of cultures inspired by mythological ancestors who even today dictate how humans must live in the forest. In the Andean Cordillera and the mountains of the Sierra Nevada de Santa Marta of Colombia we'll discover that the earth really is alive, pulsing, responsive in a thousand ways to the spiritual readiness of humankind. Dreamtime and the Songlines will lead to the melaleuca forests of Arnhem Land, as we seek to understand the subtle philosophy of the first humans to walk out of Africa, the Aboriginal peoples of

Australia. In Nepal a stone path will take us to a door that will open to reveal the radiant face of a wisdom hero, a Bodhisattva, Tsetsam Ani, a Buddhist nun who forty-five years ago entered lifelong retreat. The flight of a hornbill, like a cursive script of nature, will let us know that we have arrived at last amongst the nomadic Penan in the upland forests of Borneo.

What ultimately we will discover on this journey will be our mission for the next century. There is a fire burning over the earth, taking with it plants and animals, ancient skills and visionary wisdom. At risk is a vast archive of knowledge and expertise, a catalogue of the imagination, an oral and written language composed of the memories of countless elders and healers, warriors, farmers, fishermen, midwives, poets, and saints — in short, the artistic, intellectual, and spiritual expression of the full complexity and diversity of the human experience. Quelling this flame, this spreading inferno, and rediscovering a new appreciation for the diversity of the human spirit as expressed by culture, is among the central challenges of our times.

TWO

THE WAYFINDERS

"That's why we sail. So our children can grow up and be proud of whom they are. We are healing our souls by reconnecting to our ancestors. As we voyage we are creating new stories within the tradition of the old stories, we are literally creating a new culture out of the old." — Nainoa Thompson

LET'S SLIP FOR A MOMENT into the largest culture sphere ever brought into being by the human imagination. Polynesia: 25 million square kilometres, nearly a fifth of the surface of the planet, tens of thousands of islands flung like jewels upon the southern sea. Some months ago I was fortunate to join a good friend, Nainoa Thompson, and the Polynesian Voyaging Society on a training mission on board the *Hokule'a,* a beautiful and iconic vessel named after Arcturus, the sacred star of Hawaii. A replica of the great seafaring canoes of ancient

Polynesia, the *Hokule'a* is a double-hulled open-decked catamaran 62 feet long, 19 feet wide, lashed together by some 8 kilometres of rope, with a fully loaded displacement of some 24,000 pounds. First launched in 1975, the *Hokule'a* has since criss-crossed the Pacific, visiting over the course of some 150,000 kilometres virtually every island group of the Polynesian triangle, from Hawaii to Tahiti to the Cook Islands and beyond to Aotearoa or New Zealand, east to the Marquesas, and south and east to Rapa Nui, or Easter Island. Even more distant voyages have taken her to the coast of Alaska and the shores of Japan. The *Hokule'a* carries a crew of ten, including captain and wayfinder, two quite distinct roles. On board is not a single modern navigational aid, save a radio only to be used in case of dire emergency. There is no sextant, no depth gauge, no GPS, no transponder. There are only the multiple senses of the navigator, the knowledge of the crew, and the pride, authority, and power of an entire people reborn.

When European sailors first entered the Pacific in the sixteenth century they encountered a new planet. Among the Spaniards it was not Cortés but Vasco Núñez de Balboa who first stood silent upon a peak in Darien and with eagle eyes stared with "wild surmise" upon an ocean so vast it dwarfed the western islands, Homer's realms of gold, and all the "goodly states and kingdoms seen." The poet John Keats, writing two centuries later, imagined with awe what the first Spaniards must have felt. Ferdinand Magellan in 1520 took thirty-eight days to round the horn, the southern tip of South America, and with half his men dead, slipped into a void he took to be a peaceful sea. He sailed on, and in four months upon the water, with the surviving sailors dying by the day, he managed to miss every populated island group in the Pacific. Finally on April 7, 1521, he landed on the island of Cebu in what we now know as the Philippines. Magellan was a brave man, ruthless in many ways, but also stubborn. In his desperation and blindness he had by circumstance bypassed an entire civilization that might have taught him a great deal indeed about the open water.

The first sustained contact between Polynesians and the Spanish occurred three generations later, when in 1595 Álvaro de Mendaña de Neira, following the easterly trades, came upon an archipelago of ten volcanic islands rising as sentinels out of the equatorial sea. Before even making landfall, he named them the Marquesas, after his patron, García Hurtado de Mendoza, Marquis of Cañete, then viceroy of Peru. They comprised the most isolated island group in the world, and yet were home at the time to as many as 300,000 people who knew their islands as *Te Henua, Te Enata,* "the land of men."

It was an extraordinary meeting of civilizations. The Marquesans considered their islands to be the end of the world, the last stop on a mythical journey that had carried their ancestors along wind and waves from the west. Every human being was a descendant of Tiki, the first human, and each clan could trace its genealogical history to the primordial diaspora that had come out of the setting sun. Beyond the horizon to the east were the lands of the afterworld, where spirits departed the body and plunged into the sea. Thus, to the Marquesans, the Spaniards were as demons, embodiments of depravity born beyond the far reaches of the eastern sky. Carnal and deceitful, cruel beyond reason, the Spaniards offered nothing. They had no skills, no food or women, no knowledge of even the most fundamental elements of the natural world. Their wealth lay only in what they possessed, curious metal objects that were not without interest. But they had no understanding that true wealth was found in prestige, and that status could only be conferred upon one capable of acquiring social debts and distributing surplus food to those in need, thus guaranteeing freedom from want. The white Atua — these strangers who came from beyond all shores — had no place in the order of life. Such was their barbaric state that sorcery did not affect them, or even the power of the priests. So complete was their ignorance that they did not distinguish commoners from chiefs, even as they treated both with murderous disdain.

The Spaniards, for their part, were confounded by an island people who appeared both gentle and merciless, often in the same moment. Here were great warriors fully capable of ruthless violence. Yet their conflicts were seasonal, preconceived, scheduled, and ritualized. A single death could signal the end of battle. The Marquesans had no sense of time, no notion of sin or shame. Their young women flaunted their beauty and were openly sexual, and yet were scandalized and disgusted when the Spaniards relieved themselves in public, as any normal man would do. If sexual licentiousness titillated and confused, cannibalism and human sacrifice horrified, as did the practice of polyandry and the impossible irrationality of *tapu*, the indigenous system of magical rules and sanctions that later gave rise to the notion of taboo. Yet other signs of savagery were the glowing blue-black tattoos that covered every part of the Marquesan male body between the waist and the knees, including the most sensitive surfaces of the genitalia.

For the Spaniards the most perplexing question was how such a primitive people could have accomplished so much. Entire mountainsides and river valleys had been domesticated with monumental stone terraces, irrigation canals, and massive platforms where thousands could gather for ceremonial events, the feasts and celebrations that marked the end of war or the accession of a chief. At such moments, a priest would recite the entire mythological history of the world, hundreds of lines of sacred verse held in the memory of a single man. If he faltered or stumbled on a single phrase, he would be obliged to begin anew, for the words defined the contours of history, even as they anticipated the promise of the future. Around the platforms stretched emerald fields of taro and yams, pandanus and coconuts. The tree of life was breadfruit, and in the cool earth the Marquesans built massive stone pits where literally tons of the starchy food could be stored in anaerobic conditions, an eight-month supply held in reserve at all times, so that the people might survive even the most terrifying and destructive of typhoons.

Pedro Fernández de Queirós, second in command of the Spanish expedition, concluded that the natives he and his comrades met on the beach could not possibly have been responsible for the civilization so indelibly etched onto the land. He noted how the local women swarmed around the Spanish ships like fish because they were forbidden by tapu from using canoes. How could a culture that had no means of transporting its women settle a string of islands three months distant from the nearest outpost of the Spanish realm? How could men without benefit of a magnetic compass, which he noted they lacked, have sailed to these islands? Conflating myth with geography, he concluded that the Marquesas were in fact an outpost of a great southern continent, and that the people had been transported to the islands by an ancient civilization still waiting to be discovered. Thus, within a month of making landfall, the Spaniards sailed on into the Pacific, searching for this legendary land, a futile quest that would consume the rest of Fernández de Queirós's life.

QUEIRÓS WAS NOT the last sailor to be misled and confounded by the enigma of Polynesia. At a time when European transports, lacking navigational instruments to measure longitude, hugged the coastlines of continents for fear of the open ocean, accounts trickled back to Paris and Amsterdam of fleets of curious vessels plying the open waters of the Pacific. In 1616 a Dutch naval ship sailing between Tonga and Samoa came upon a flotilla of massive seagoing trading canoes. In 1714, when a mansion in London could be fully furnished for hundred pounds, the British government through an act of Parliament offered a prize of 20,000 British pounds to anyone who could solve the problem of determining longitude. Until the invention of the chronometer, navigators relied on dead reckoning, which made it hazardous for an ordinary ship to sail beyond sight of land. Yet in the Pacific something exceptional was going on.

Captain James Cook, arguably the finest navigator in the history of the Royal Navy, was the first to pay serious notice. When he landed in Hawaii, his flagship was met by a flotilla of 3,000 native canoes. At Tonga, he observed that local catamarans could cover three leagues in the time it took his ship to achieve two. He encountered men from the Marquesas who could understand the language of Tahitians, though nearly 1,600 kilometres separated these islands. On his very first voyage in 1769 he met in Tahiti a navigator and priest, Tupaia, who drew a map from memory of every major island group in Polynesia, save Hawaii and Aotearoa. More than 120 stones were placed in the sand, each a symbol of an island across a span of more than 4,000 kilometres from the Marquesas in the east to Fiji in the west, a distance equal to the width of the continental United States.

Tupaia later sailed with Cook from Tahiti to New Zealand, a circuitous journey of nearly 13,000 kilometres that ranged between 48 degrees south latitude and 4 degrees north. To his astonishment, Cook reported, the Polynesian navigator was able to indicate, at every moment of the voyage, the precise direction back to Tahiti, though he had neither benefit of sextant nor knowledge of charts.

Cook and his naturalist, Joseph Banks, who both learned Tahitian, recognized the obvious cultural connections between the distant islands. Linguistic evidence suggested to Banks that the people of the Pacific had originated in the East Indies. Cook, too, was convinced that the settling of Polynesia had occurred from the west. From Tupaia he had learned certain secrets of the winds, how to follow the sun by day and the stars by night, and he was enormously impressed when the navigator described in detail sailing directions from Tahiti to Samoa and Fiji, south to Australia, and east all the way to the Marquesas. But he never could quite convince himself that these journeys had been purposeful. He knew the fury of the Pacific, and had encountered a group of Tahitians who, helpless in the face of a headwind, had drifted hundreds of kilometres off course, only to be marooned for months in the Cook Islands.

Thus began a debate that spun over the waters for almost two centuries. Who really were these people? Where had they come from? And how had they reached across an ocean to settle these impossibly remote and isolated lands? In 1832 the French explorer Dumont d'Urville classified the peoples of the Pacific into three categories. Micronesians inhabited the small atolls of the western Pacific north of the equator. Melanesians dwelt in the "dark islands" of New Guinea, the Solomons, Vanuatu, New Caledonia and Fiji. Polynesia encompassed what remained, the "many islands" of the eastern Pacific. Micronesia, named for the size of the islands, and Melanesia, named for the colour of its inhabitants' skin, were both arbitrary designations. They linger to this day despite having no historical or ethnographic justification. But in distinguishing the people of Polynesia, Dumont d'Urville recognized what every captain's log had recorded: There was effectively a single cultural realm of closely related languages and shared historical vision spread across an entire ocean, with the most extreme points separated one from one another by a distance equal to twice the width of Canada. That the Polynesians had occupied these islands was self-evident. Explanations for how they had done so exemplified what the poet Walt Whitman meant when he wrote that history is the swindle of the schoolmasters.

As early as 1803, citing the impossibility of sailing east into the prevailing winds, Joaquín Martinez de Zuniga, a Spanish priest stationed in the Philippines, identified South America as the place of Polynesian origins. A little while later, John Lang, an influential clergyman in the early days of the Australian colony of New South Wales, first suggested the notion of "accidental drift," accepting that Polynesians had settled the islands from the west, but only by chance, hapless sailors blown off course, fishermen who went out for food only to stumble upon new lands. This notion of serendipitous diffusion defied logic — after all, what fisherman takes to sea his entire domestic tool kit, chickens, pigs, dogs, taro, bananas, yams, not to mention his family — but as an explanation it had the convenience of acknowledging historical facts while denying Polynesian people what we now know to have been their greatest achievement. Accidental drift, championed in particular by a New Zealand civil servant, Andrew Sharp, was not laid to rest until the early 1970s, when a series of sophisticated computer simulations, based on naval hydrographic records of wind and currents, concluded that out of 16,000 simulated drift voyages from various points in eastern Polynesia, not one had managed to reach Hawaii.

The waters were further muddied, if you will, by two men, both of whom saw the world not as it was but as they would have liked it to be. Sir Peter Buck was born Te Rangi Hiroa, son of a Maori mother and an Irish father. One of the most prominent Polynesian scholars of the mid-twentieth century, he headed for many years the Bishop Museum in Honolulu, and by association held an influential professorship at Yale. Acutely sensitive to his mixed heritage, and keen in the era of Jim Crow to distinguish Polynesians from the "Negroid" races, he elaborated a theory that the Pacific had been settled from

Asia in a wave of deliberate migrations that swept through the islands, but completely bypassed Melanesia. Though this ran contrary to geography and ignored the fact that nearly all Polynesian crop plants were of Melanesian origin, it did allow Buck to claim that: "the master mariners of the Pacific must be Europoid for they are not characterized by the wooly hair, black skins, and thin lower legs of the Negroids nor by the flat face, short stature, and drooping inner eyefold of the Mongoloids."

If Peter Buck's racial uncertainties distorted his lens on history, a young Norwegian zoologist, Thor Heyerdahl, inverted history itself with the claim, supported by a harrowing journey of some 7,000 kilometres on a balsa raft, that Polynesia had actually been settled from South America. When the raft, named *Kon-Tiki*, crashed onto a reef in the Raroia Atoll in the Tuamotus some 800 kilometres northeast of Tahiti on August 7, 1947, after a 101-day journey from Peru, a *National Geographic* hero was born. Heyerdahl was blond, good-looking, bronzed by the sun, charismatic, and eminently photogenic: the very archetype of the modern adventurer. His argument in favour of American origins for the people of the Pacific, however, was dubious in the extreme.

The argument was based on three strands of non-evidence. First, Heyerdahl maintained, as had the early Spaniards, that it would have been impossible for Polynesians to sail east into the prevailing equatorial winds. This was an old puzzle that had in fact been solved by Captain Cook in his conversations with the navigator

Tupaia. The answer was an open secret in Polynesia, but perhaps unknown to Heyerdahl, or at least inconvenient for his hypothesis. There is a time every year when the trade winds reverse, and sailors are free to sail east, knowing full well that if they become lost, they need only await the returning easterlies to carry them home.

Heyerdahl's second argument focused on monumental architecture. Comparing the stonework of the Inca with that of Polynesia, he cited similarities so superficial as to be meaningless to the trained eye of an archaeologist. Third, and the only interesting possibility, was the presence in Polynesia of the sweet potato, *Ipomoea batatas,* a plant undoubtedly of American origin. All this implied, as we now know, was that Polynesian vessels reached South America and returned home, a fact corroborated by the recent discovery of chicken bones, a bird of Asian origin, in pre-Columbian middens at El Arenal, on the south coast of Chile.

In making his sensational claim Thor Heyerdahl ignored the overwhelming body of linguistic, ethnographic, and ethnobotanical evidence, augmented today by genetic and archaeological data, indicating that he was patently wrong. He failed to note that in order to get *Kon-Tiki* beyond the Humboldt Current at the beginning of its voyage he had required the aid of the Peruvian navy. Or that there was no evidence in his time, or today, to suggest that the design of sail rigged on the raft existed in pre-Columbian South America. Indeed, Heyerdahl was so loose with his interpretations, and so casual with chronology, that his theory, as one scholar has suggested, was equivalent to a modern historian claiming that: "America was discovered in the last days of the Roman Empire by King Henry VIII, who brought a Ford Thunderbird to the benighted aborigines." But none of this mattered. Heyerdahl's story was a sensation and his book, *Kon-Tiki,* went on to sell more than 20 million copies.

FOR POLYNESIANS AND serious scholars of Polynesia, Heyerdahl's theory, which denied the culture its greatest accomplishment, was the ultimate insult. But it inspired two vitally important initiatives. First, it forced archaeologists to dig, to seek and find concrete evidence that would allow them to trace the Polynesian diaspora. Second, it led Hawaiians to sail. The Polynesian Voyaging Society, established in 1973, launched the *Hokule'a* on March 8, 1975. What began as a visionary experiment grew over time into a mission to recapture history and reclaim a stolen legacy.

The challenge for archaeologists had always been the dearth of physical remains upon which to establish a chronology. Polynesians, technically sophisticated in so many ways, at the time of European contact did not use pottery. A first breakthrough came in 1952 on New Caledonia in the Coral Sea. There, at a remote site near a beach called Lapita, archaeologists did find pottery, highly distinctive stamped ceramics identical to shards that had been found thirty years before on Tonga, an island 2,400 kilometres to the east. Subsequent discoveries in New Guinea and Vanuatu, Fiji and the Solomon Islands left no doubt of the existence of a lost civilization, an ancient cultural sphere that, beginning around 1500 BC, had spread from Melanesia east into the Pacific. In one of the great sagas of prehistory, a people known to us as Lapita, named for the original site in New Caledonia, had left their original home in the forests of New Guinea and set out to settle a world. Within five centuries, perhaps twenty generations, and sailing against the prevailing winds, they crossed 3,200 kilometres of water to reach not only Fiji but beyond, to Samoa and Tonga. And they made this journey ten centuries before the birth of Christ.

Then, for reasons that remain unknown, the movement rested for nearly a thousand years. The ceramic tradition was lost, but not syntax and grammar, the meaning of carved stone or the decorated body, the power of the ancestors and the divine origins of the wind. Beginning around 200 BC, a new wave of exploration began, inspired by the direct ancestors of modern Polynesians. From Samoa and Tonga they sailed east, reaching the Cook Islands, Tahiti, and the Marquesas, a distance of some 4,000 kilometres. Then, after another hiatus of centuries, new discoveries were made, first Rapa Nui, or Easter Island, and then Hawaii, which was settled by AD 400. The final great phase of the Polynesian diaspora unfolded roughly around the time of the First Crusade, as navigators probed to the south and west, making landfall in Aotearoa, later New Zealand, around AD 1000. Five centuries before Columbus, the Polynesians had over the course of only eighty generations settled virtually every island group of the Pacific, establishing a single sphere of cultural life encompassing some 25 million square kilometres of the earth's surface.

Imagine for a moment what these journeys entailed. The sailors travelled in open catamarans, all built with tools made from coral, stone, and human bone. Their sails were woven from pandanus, the planking sewn together with cordage spun from coconut fibre; cracks were sealed with breadfruit sap and resins. Exposed to the elements, the sun by day, the cold wind by night, with hunger and thirst as constant companions, these people crossed thousands of kilometres of ocean, discovering hundreds of new lands, some the size of small continents, others mere island atolls less than a kilometre in diameter with no landmarks higher than a coconut tree.

While no doubt there were instances of fishermen blown out to sea or stranded by the wind as they sailed offshore in pursuit of schools of pelagic fish, the overwhelming evidence suggests that these voyages were deliberate and purposeful journeys of discovery. But why did they go? Why would anyone risk his or her life to leave a place like Tahiti or Rarotonga to head into a void? Prestige, curiosity, a spirit of adventure certainly played a role. To sail off into the rising sun, quite possibly never to be seen again, was an act of considerable courage that brought enormous honour to a clan. Oral traditions suggest that as many as half of these expeditions may have ended in disaster. But as failure implied death, those left behind had a vested interest in imagining success, and in their dreams they envisioned new lands rising out of the sea to greet their departed relatives, men and women who acquired by their very acts the status of gods.

As in any culture, there were more mundane motivations. Inheritance in Polynesia was based on primogeniture, and the social structure was fiercely hierarchical. The only way for a second or third son, or the scion of a lowly family or clan, to achieve wealth and status was to find a new world. Ecological imperatives and crises, both natural and man-made, also drove discovery. The pollen record on Rapa Nui, or Easter Island, suggests that until the arrival of Polynesians the island was densely covered in subtropical forest. By the time of European contact the landscape had been completely modified, with many local species driven to extinction, and much of the wealth of the soil exhausted. The flightless birds of New Zealand disappeared within a generation of settlement. Polynesians were fully capable of overexploiting the natural world, and when their populations exceeded the carrying capacity of the land, they had no choice but to move on. This implied heading out to sea.

Whatever the ultimate motivation, the ancient Polynesians sailed. And though many of the voyages were indeed exploratory, and certain remote islands such as Rapa Nui, once settled, may have become over time isolated, these were not all one-way journeys of desperation. To the contrary, all evidence suggests that regular long-distance trade along established routes crisscrossed the ocean.

But how did the Polynesians do it? They left no written records. Theirs were oral traditions, with all knowledge stored in memory, transmitted generation to generation. One of the tragedies of history was the failure of early Europeans, with notable exceptions such as Captain Cook, to make any effort to study and record, let alone celebrate, this extraordinary repository of seafaring knowledge. The prestige and authority of the traditional navigators should have been evident to any unbiased observer; they were the cultural pivots of every community. Navigation fundamentally defined the Polynesian identity. That these masters were ignored was no mere oversight, but an inevitable consequence of the clash of cultures that came with conquest.

Contact brought chaos and devastation. The two pillars of Polynesian society, aside from the navigators, were the chief and the priest. The authority of the chief was based on his capacity to control and distribute surplus food. The power of the priest lay in a spiritual capacity to enforce tapu, the sacred rules of the culture. When European diseases swept through the islands, killing up to 85 percent of the people on the Marquesas in less than a month, the demographic collapse destroyed the traditional economy, even as it compromised the priests, who had no capacity to sanction foreigners who violated tapu with impunity and by some miracle were immune to pestilence. Missionaries, who in considerable numbers crossed the beaches in the wake of sustained contact, blamed the people themselves for their misfortunes, even as they dismissed their religious beliefs as crude idolatry. In such an atmosphere, it would have been difficult indeed for Europeans to acknowledge that Polynesians possessed navigational skills that rivalled and even surpassed those of their own sailors, especially given that seamanship, particularly in Britain, was the pride of the nation. But they most assuredly did.

TO UNDERSTAND THE GENIUS of the ancient Polynesians, Nainoa Thompson told me on the deck of the *Hokule'a* as we left Kauai in a fierce rain to round Oahu before heading north from Molokai by night to the open sea, you must begin with the fundamental elements of the Polynesian world: wind, waves, clouds, stars, sun, moon, birds, fish, and the water itself. Bring to these the raw power of empirical observation, of universal human inquiry. The skills of the traditional navigator are not unlike those of the scientist; one learns through direct experience and the testing of hypotheses, with information drawn from all branches of the natural sciences, astronomy, animal behaviour, meteorology, and oceanography. Temper this with a lifelong training of impossibly intense commitment and discipline, all to be rewarded with the highest level of prestige in a culture where status counted for everything. All the intellectual brilliance of humanity, in other words, together with the full potential of human desire and ambitions, was applied to the challenge of the sea.

Nainoa's teacher for more than thirty years was Mau Piailug, a master navigator from Satawal in the Caroline Islands of Micronesia. Mau grew up on a coral islet less than 1.5 square kilometres, a third the size of Central Park in New York. His universe was the ocean. His grandfather was a navigator, and his father before him. At the age of one Mau was selected to inherit the ancestral teachings. As part of that training he was placed as an infant in tidal pools for hours at a time that he might feel and absorb the rhythms of the sea. When, at eight, on his first deep ocean voyage, he became sick from the swells, his teacher's solution was to tie him to a rope and drag him behind the canoe until the nausea passed. As a young man of fourteen he tied his testicles to the rigging of the vessel to more carefully sense the movement of the canoe through the water. Mau learned not only to sail, but also to understand the secrets of the Big Water, both the physics and metaphysics of waves. It was said he could conjure islands out of the sea just by holding a vision of them in his imagination.

In the shadow of Mau's achievements, Nainoa, a young Hawaiian from a disenfranchised noble family whose grandmother had been beaten at mission school for speaking her native language, found hope and aspired to greatness. From Mau he learned to pay attention to weather, to read the waves, to understand the meaning of stars — as he put it, to plot a chart to an island in his mind.

The prevailing trade winds do indeed come out of the east, Nainoa told me, but they do not dominate in the simple manner envisioned by Thor Heyerdahl and others. As the navigator Tupaia once explained to Captain Cook, there is a time each year when the winds reverse, and westerly breezes blow across the Pacific. A trough of low pressure forms a corridor running east from northern Australia, the very route along which the Lapita civilization migrated from the Bismarck Archipelago into the central Pacific. Similarly, farther north, closer to Hawaii, the winds do not consistently and only blow from the east. What's more, as the *Hokule'a* has proven over the course of more than a dozen deep ocean voyages, it is possible to tack into the wind, even with a fully loaded canoe.

The ancient Polynesians, Nainoa added, were not navigators in a modern sense so much as wayfinders. Sailing from Tahiti for Oahu, for example, they did not set course for Pearl Harbor; they set out to find a chain of islands, the Hawaiian Archipelago. Moreover, the distances in the Pacific are not as formidable as they appear on a chart. With the exception of the three most distant points of the Polynesian Triangle, Rapa Nui, Hawaii and Aotearoa (New Zealand), no voyage from Melanesia through Polynesia has to traverse more than 500 kilometres of open water, at least as the crow flies. And there is more land than the maps reveal. At sea one can see roughly 50 kilometres in any direction. Draw a circle with a radius of 50 kilometres around every landfall, and suddenly the ocean shrinks and the area effectively "covered" by land increases.

Clouds also provide clues to the wayfinder — their shape, colour, character, and place in the sky. Brown clouds bring strong winds; high clouds no wind but lots of rain. Their movements reveal the strength and direction of winds, the stability of the sky, the volatility of storm fronts. There is an entire nomenclature to describe the distinct patterns clouds form as they gather over islands or sweep across the open ocean. Light alone can be read, the rainbow colours at the edge of stars, the way they twinkle and dim with an impending storm, the tone of the sky over an island, always darker than that over open sea. Red skies at sunrise and sunset indicate humidity in the air. A halo around the moon foreshadows rain, for it is caused by light shining through ice crystals of clouds laden with moisture. The number of stars within the halo anticipates the intensity of the storm; if there are fewer than ten, expect trouble, high winds, and torrential rain. If a double halo surrounds the moon the weather will move in on the wings of a gale.

Other signs are found in wildlife and seamarks, as opposed to landmarks. A tan shark moving lazily in the sea. A lone bird separated from its flock. Dolphins and porpoises swimming toward sheltered waters herald a storm, while the flight of a frigate bird heading out to sea anticipates calm. Pelagic birds like the albatross lead nowhere, but others such as petrels and terns travel fixed distances from their nests, returning every night to land, rising out of the waves at sunset, their flight paths home as precise as compass bearings. A sighting of a white tern indicates that land is within 200 kilometres; the brown tern reaches out as far as 65 kilometres, the boobies rarely more than 40. Phosphorescence and the debris of plants in the sea, the salinity and taste and temperature of the water, the manner in which a swordfish swims, all these become revelatory in the senses of the navigator.

All of this made sense until we rounded the backside of Molokai and in the darkness of night sailed north into the face of a distant storm. As Nainoa told me, it was one thing to know what to look for, these clues and signs and indications; it was quite another to pull it altogether and confront in the moment the ever-changing power and reality of the sea.

The sky was still clear, the ocean black, the heavens dominated by the innumerable silences of the stars. The *Hokule'a* lumbered into the swells, which were moderate, but still strong, enough to heave the deck and obliterate, to my eye at least, any sense of a horizon. The crew worked in two-hour shifts, with everyone taking a turn at the helm, which was not a rudder but a long steering paddle that took three to handle. Enshrouded by the night, the canoe itself became the needle of a compass that was the sky. Behind us sat the navigator, a young woman named Ka'iulani, Nainoa's protege. She would remain awake for twenty-two hours a day for the entire voyage, sleeping only for fleeting moments when the mind demanded a rest.

Ka'iulani, like Nainoa and all of the experienced crew, could name and follow some 220 stars in the night sky. She knew and could track all the constellations, Scorpio and the Southern Cross, Orion, the Pleiades and the North Star, Polaris. But for her the most important stars were those low in the sky, the ones that had just risen or were about to set. Nainoa explained: As the Earth rotates, every star comes up over the eastern horizon, describes an arc through the sky, and then sets on a westerly bearing. These two points on the horizon, where a specific star rises in the east and sets in the west, remain the same throughout the year, though the time at which a star emerges changes by four minutes every night. Thus, as long as one is able to commit to memory all the stars and their unique positions, the time at which each is to appear on a particular night, and their bearings as they break the horizon or slip beneath it, one can envision a 360-degree compass, which the Hawaiians divide conceptually into the thirty-two star houses, each a segment on the horizon named for a celestial body. Any one star is only dependable for a time, for as it arcs through the sky its bearings change. But by then there will be another star breaking the horizon, again on a bearing known to the navigator. Over the course of a night at sea — roughly twelve hours in the tropics — ten such guiding stars are enough to maintain a course. To steer, the crew at the helm, instructed by the navigator, takes advantage of the canoe itself, positioning the vessel so that a particular star or celestial body remains framed, for example, within the angle subtended between the top of the mast and stays that support it. Any consistent point of reference will do.

With the dawn comes the sun, always a critical transition for the navigator. It is a moment to take measure of the sea and sky, study the winds, and observe their impact on the waves. Mau, Nainoa's teacher, had dozens of names just to identify the different widths and colours caused by the path of the sun as its light and shadow rose and moved over water. All of these told him something about the day to come.

The stern of the *Hokule'a* is square, which allows the navigator readily to orient to east and west at both sunset and break of day. There are eight marks incised along the railings on both sides of the vessel, each paired to a single point in the stern, giving bearings in two directions, fore and aft — thirty-two bearings altogether, which correspond to the thirty-two directional houses of the star compass. The navigator by day conceptually divides the horizon ahead and behind, each into sixteen parts, taking as cardinal points the rising and setting of the sun. Thus by day he or she replicates the star compass of the night. The metaphor is that the *Hokule'a* never moves. It simply waits, the axis mundi of the world, as the islands rise out of the sea to greet her.

Beyond sun and stars is the ocean itself. When clouds or mist obliterate the horizon, the navigator must orient the vessel by the feel of the water, distinguishing waves created by local weather systems, for example, from the swells generated by pressure systems far beyond the horizon. And these swells, in turn, must be differentiated from the deep ocean currents that run through the Pacific, and which can be followed with the same ease with which a terrestrial explorer would follow a river to its mouth. Expert navigators like Mau, sitting alone in the darkness of the hull of a canoe, can sense and distinguish as many as five distinct swells moving through the vessel at any given time. Local wave action is chaotic and disruptive. But the distant swells are consistent, deep and resonant pulses that move across the ocean from one star house to another, 180 degrees away, and thus can be used as yet another means of orienting the vessel in time and space. Should the canoe shift course in the middle of the night, the navigator will know, simply from the change of the pitch and roll of the waves. Even more remarkable is the navigator's ability to pull islands out of the sea. The truly great navigators such as Mau can identify the presence of distant atolls of islands beyond the visible horizon simply by watching the reverberation of waves across the hull of the canoe, knowing full well that every island group in the Pacific has its own refractive pattern that can be read with the same ease with which a forensic scientist would read a fingerprint.

All of this is extraordinary, each one of these individual skills and intuitions a sign of a certain brilliance.

But as we isolate, deconstruct, even celebrate these specific intellectual and observational gifts, we run the risk of missing the entire point, for the genius of Polynesian navigation lies not in the particular but in the whole, the manner in which all of these points of information come together in the mind of the wayfinder. It is one thing, for example, to measure the speed of the *Hokule'a* with a simple calculation: the time a bit of foam or flotsam, or perhaps a mere bubble, takes to pass the known length separating the crossbeams of the canoe. Three seconds and the speed will be 8.5 knots; fifteen seconds and the vessel slogs at a mere 1.5 knots.

But it is quite another to make such calculations continually, day and night, while also taking the measure of stars breaking the horizon, winds shifting both in speed and direction, swells moving through the canoe, clouds and waves. The science and art of navigation is holistic. The navigator must process an endless flow of data, intuitions and insights derived from observation and the dynamic rhythms and interactions of wind, waves, clouds, stars, sun, moon, the flight of birds, a bed of kelp, the glow of phosphorescence on a shallow reef — in short, the constantly changing world of weather and the sea.

What is even more astonishing is that the entire science of wayfinding is based on dead reckoning. You only know where you are by knowing precisely where you have been and how you got to where you are. One's position at any one time is determined solely on the basis of distance and direction travelled since leaving the last known point. "You don't look up at the stars and know where you are," Nainoa told me, "you need to know where you have come from by memorizing from where you sailed."

It was the impossibility of keeping track over a long voyage of every shift in speed, current, and bearing that kept European sailors hugging the coastlines before the problem of longitude was solved with invention of the chronometer. But this is precisely what the Polynesians managed to do, and all without benefit of the written word. There were no logs, notebooks, or charts, no speedometers, watches, or compasses. Every bit of data — wind, currents, speed, direction, distance, time — acquired over the course of a deep sea voyage, including the sequence of its acquisition, had to be stored within the memory of one person, the navigator. Latitude north and south could always be determined from the stars, but not longitude. Should the navigator lose the position in relationship to the reference course, the vessel would be lost. This is why Ka'iulani, like all wayfinders, did not sleep over the course of our short journey. Navigators do not sleep. They remain monk-like, undisturbed by the crew, with no mundane tasks to perform, sitting alone on a special perch at the stern of the vessel, tracking with their minds.

"If you can read the ocean," Mau once told Nainoa, "if you can see the island in your mind, you will never get lost."

In 1976, on its first deep sea voyage, the *Hokule'a* under Mau's guidance sailed from Hawaii 4,400 kilometres to Tahiti, where it was greeted, quite unexpectedly, by an enormous, jubilant crowd of over 16,000. Nothing like this had ever been seen in French Polynesia. The colonial administrators, as long ago as the mid-eighteen hundreds, had formally outlawed virtually every aspect of traditional cultural life, including long-distance oceanic trade between the islands. The *Hokule'a* brought everything back to life, as if the wind itself were whispers coming forward in time.

In 1999, having criss-crossed the Pacific from Marquesas and to Aotearoa, the Polynesian Voyaging Society embarked on its most ambitious journey. With Nainoa as navigator, the *Hokule'a* would try to pull Rapa Nui out of the sea. It was a wildly ambitious expedition. The distance from Hawaii to Easter Island is roughly 10,000 kilometres, but the journey implies crossing the Doldrums and tacking into the wind for 2,300 kilometres, which effectively doubles the total sailing distance to nearly 20,000 kilometres. And all to make landfall on an island 23 kilometres in diameter, less than a single degree on a compass, had in fact a compass been on board. Food and water rations were cut in half to lighten the load. In dry dock 4,000 pounds were stripped from the vessel. The crew was the smallest ever to sail the *Hokule'a*. The route went via the Marquesas to Pitcairn Island. From there they would tack south, pick up the westerly winds, and sail east and north until within a distance from their target roughly equivalent to the length of the Hawaiian Archipelago. Then they would search for the island, sailing back and forth in a grid, careful that on the downwind runs to the west they would not overshoot and find themselves forced by the winds to sail on for South America.

At one point, close to their goal, Nainoa snapped awake in a daze and realized that with the overcast skies and the sea fog, he had no idea where they were. He had lost the continuity of mind and memory essential to survival at sea. He masked his fear from the crew and in despair remembered Mau's words. *Can you see the image of the island in your mind?* He became calm, and realized that he had already found the island. It was the *Hokule'a*, and he had everything he needed on board the sacred canoe. Suddenly, the sky brightened and a beam of warm light appeared on his shoulder. The clouds cleared and he followed that beam directly to the island of Rapa Nui.

I found it an extraordinary experience to sail with Nainoa on the *Hokule'a* along with the crew from the Polynesian Voyaging Society. As important as Mau was to him as a mentor and guide, Nainoa Thompson has become an icon for an entire generation of young Polynesians, an immensely important cultural figure, publicly more admired than anyone else in Hawaii. There is a strong sense throughout the islands that as long as the *Hokule'a* sails the culture of the navigators will survive. Nainoa's entire mission in life is to ensure that this happens. He refers to *Hokule'a* as both a sacred canoe and the spaceship of the ancestors. To me, this is a fitting choice of words. Indeed, if you took all of the genius that has allowed us to put a man on the moon and applied it to an understanding of the ocean, what you would get is Polynesia.

I AM DRAWN TO the story of Polynesia because it reveals so much about the issues and misconceptions that both inspire and haunt us to this day: the sheer courage that true exploration implies, the brilliance of human adaptation, the dark impact of conquest and colonialism. It reminds us, too, of the need always to be skeptical about the tenacious grip of academic orthodoxy. Knowledge is rarely completely divorced from power, and interpretation is too often an expression of convenience.

Anthropology, as we saw in the first lecture, grew out of an evolutionary model in which nineteenth-century men such Lewis Henry Morgan and Herbert Spencer envisioned societies as stages in a linear progression of advancement, leading, as they conceived it, from savagery to barbarism to civilization. Each of these phases of human development was correlated, in their calculations, with specific technological innovations. Fire, ceramics, and the bow and arrow marked the savage. With the domestication of animals, the rise of agriculture, and the invention of metalworking, we entered the level of the barbarian. Literacy implied civilization. Every society, it was assumed, progressed through the same stages, in the same sequence. Thus the technological sophistication of a people placed them on a particular step on the ladder rising toward evolutionary success.

The Polynesians and the British may have been contemporaries, but the lack of guns and cannon implied that the former were at an earlier juncture in their evolution, while the sailors of Captain Cook represented a later and more advanced stage.

Such a transparently simplistic and biased interpretation of human history, though long repudiated by anthropologists as an intellectual artifact of the nineteenth century, as relevant today as the convictions of Victorian clergy who dated the earth at a mere 6,000 years, has nevertheless proved to be remarkably persistent, even among contemporary scholars. A recent Canadian book, *Disrobing the Aboriginal Industry: The Deception Behind Indigenous Cultural Preservation*, ridicules the notion that indigenous inhabitants of the Americas had anything of interest to offer the world at the time of first European encounter. "Never in history," the authors write, "has the cultural gap between two peoples coming into contact with each other been wider. It doesn't mean," they add helpfully, referring in a phrase to tens of millions of people speaking perhaps as many as three thousand languages, "that [indigenous people] are stupid or inferior. We all passed through the stage of Neolithic culture." That such a sentiment could be expressed by a university professor, and then seized upon by the national media as proof of the hoax of the aspirations of First Nations peoples today, is disturbing.

The Americas gave Europe tobacco, the potato and the tomato, maize, peanuts, chocolate, peppers, squash, pineapples, and the sweet potato. From the New World came quinine to treat malaria, the muscle relaxant d-Tubocurarine derived from Amazonian arrow poisons, and cocaine from the plant known to the Inca as the Divine Leaf of Immortality. These three drugs profoundly impacted Western medicine; cinchona bark, the source of quinine, alone saved tens of thousands of lives. Europe offered to the Americas wheat, barley, oats, goats, cows, African slavery, and steel, as well as typhus, malaria, measles, influenza, smallpox, and the plague. Ninety percent of the Amerindian population died within a generation or two of contact.

The Aztec capital of Tenochtitlán dazzled the early Spaniards, as did Cusco, the Inca city of gold. No place in Spain, by all contemporary accounts, could compare to either capital. The empire of the Inca only existed because it guaranteed freedom from want and starvation. Storehouse complexes distributed along the spine of the Andes held in reserve hundreds of thousands of bushels of quinoa, maize, *lisas, oca, añu,* and vast amounts of *chuño,* the world's first freeze-dried food, fabricated from any number of the 3,000 varieties of potatoes domesticated by the pre-Columbian civilizations of South America.

In contrast, four centuries after the Conquest, London was the centre of the European world, the wealthiest and most powerful city on earth. But the death rate on one side of town was twice that of the other. One in five children died in birth. The children of the poor, on average, were 6 inches shorter and 11 pounds lighter than the offspring of the rich, according to the records of the British Army. Jack London, describing the urban life of the great capital in 1901, at the height of its prestige and technological superiority, writes of the poor scrambling over heaps of hospital garbage, scraps piled high, "on a huge platter in an indescribable mess — pieces of bread, chunks of grease and fat pork, the burnt skin from the outside of roasted joints, bones, in short, all the leavings from the fingers and mouths of sick ones suffering all manner of diseases. Into this mess the men plunged their hands, digging, pawing, turning over, examining, rejecting and scrambling for food. It wasn't pretty. Pigs couldn't have done worse. But the poor devils were hungry."

There was one scholar in the early history of anthropology who recognized the inadequacies of broad theories of culture concocted by men who never went to the field and whose ideas about human advancement were obviously skewed by preconception. Franz Boas was a physicist, trained in Germany a generation before Einstein. His doctoral studies concerned the optical properties of water, and throughout his investigations his research was plagued by problems of perception, which came to fascinate him. In the eclectic way of the best of nineteenth-century scholarship, inquiry in one academic field led to another. What was the nature of knowing? Who decided what was to be known? Boas became interested in how seemingly random beliefs and convictions converged into this thing called "*culture*," a term that he was the first to promote as an organizing principle, a useful point of intellectual departure. Far ahead of his time, he sensed that every distinct social community, every cluster of people distinguished by language or adaptive inclination, was a unique facet of the human legacy and its promise.

Boas became the father of modern cultural anthropology, the first scholar to attempt to explore in a truly open and neutral manner how human social perceptions are formed, and how members of distinct societies become conditioned to see and interpret the world. Working first among the Inuit of Baffin Island and later along the Northwest coast of Canada, he insisted that his students learn and conduct their research in the language of the place and participate fully, to the extent possible, in the daily lives of the people they studied. Every effort should be made, he argued, to understand the perspective of the other, to learn the way they perceive the world, and if at all possible, the very nature of their thoughts. This demanded, by definition, a willingness to step back from the constraints of one's own prejudices and preconceptions. This notion of cultural relativism was a radical departure, as unique in its way as was Einstein's theory of relativity in the discipline of physics. Everything Boas proposed ran against orthodoxy. It was a shattering of the European mind, and ever since, anthropologists have periodically been accused of embracing an extreme relativism, as if every human behaviour must be accepted simply because it exists. In truth, no serious anthropologist advocates the elimination of judgment. Anthropology merely calls for its suspension, so that the judgments we are all ethically obliged to make as human beings may be informed ones.

For Franz Boas, the moment of epiphany came in the winter of 1883 during his first ethnographic trip to Baffin Island. Caught in a winter blizzard in temperatures that dropped to minus 46 degrees Celsius, his party became disoriented in the darkness. For twenty-six hours they pounded on by sled, Boas abandoning his fate to his Inuk companion and the dogs. Eventually they secured shelter, "half frozen and half starved." Boas was glad to be alive. The following morning he wrote in his diary, "I often ask myself what advantages our good society possesses over that of the 'savages' and find, the more I see of their customs, that we have no right to look down on them.... We have no right to blame them for their forms and superstitions which may seem ridiculous to us. We highly educated people are much worse, relatively speaking."

Boas established the template for ethnographic research, and his example inspired those who would go on to create the modern discipline of anthropology. The goal of the anthropologist is "to grasp the native's point of view, his relation to life, to realize his vision of his world." These words, which could have come from Boas, were actually written forty years later by Bronislaw Malinowski, an aristocratic Pole at the London School of Economics, who had taken ethnographic fieldwork to quite another level of commitment. At a time when economics implied the theories of either Karl Marx or Adam Smith, Malinowski turned everything upside down, challenging conventional ideas about the nature of wealth, and the purpose and meaning of exchange, even as he revealed the dynamics of a contemporary oceanic trading network so vast and complex that it offered clues as to the very forces that ultimately led to the settlement of the Pacific Ocean.

Stranded in Melanesia by the outbreak of the First World War, Malinowski had spent two years in the Trobriand Islands, an archipelago of flat coral reefs and islands located some 250 kilometres northeast of Papua New Guinea. The inhabitants, perhaps 10,000 at the time, were, in his words, "merry, talkative and easy going," with artistic skills that placed them "culturally, in the first rank of Melanesian tribes." A gifted linguist, Malinowski quickly mastered their language and went to work, readily discerning the broad outlines of the culture.

The people lived in villages, and were largely dependent on their gardens, with the primary crop being the yam, the cultivation and harvest of which determined the ebb and flow of the social and ritual cycles of the year. Descent was matrilineal. There were four recognized clans, who had birds, animals, and plants as linked totems. The islands were divided into a number of political units, each dominated by a male leader. Though conflict was endemic, wars had precise rules and battles were mostly theatrical displays of spears and shields.

The division between men and women struck Malinowski as curiously equitable. Women had considerable influence, controlled elements of the economy through their labour, and worked their own forms of magic which had nothing to do with seduction, though sex became something of an obsession for Malinowski. Inevitably a product of his own world, he was stunned by the freedom enjoyed by young Trobriand maidens. Before marriage, anything seemed to go. Once formally wed, fidelity was highly prized, and adultery severely sanctioned. Malinowski reflected upon this at length in one of the two books he wrote based on his time on the islands. His second book, however, is the one that concerns us, *Argonauts of the Western Pacific*, for this tells the story of the sea.

Malinowski reached the Trobriand Islands by boat, after a journey across violent currents and an open ocean that would have impressed any child of Kraków, the landlocked Polish city of his birth. He wanted to know how people could possibly maintain social connections across such barriers. While the Trobriand Islanders drew their subsistence almost exclusively from the land, their commerce moved over water. But, thought Malinowski, on the face of it nothing they produced could rationalize the risks even of the single voyage he had endured to reach them. It soon became clear to him that something was going on that had nothing to do with practicality, a curious system of exchange in which nothing of evident worth or value moved at great risk and with the promise of immense prestige. The Trobriand Islands, he discovered, were just one of many points in a trading network that linked scores of communities over thousands of square kilometres of ocean, small huddled clusters of humanity that clung to coral reefs and spread over the remains of sunken mountains.

Known as the Kula ring, it was a system of balanced reciprocity based on the ceremonial exchange of two items, necklaces of discs chiselled from red spondylus shells known as the *soulava,* and arm bands of white cone shell, the *mwali.* These were strictly symbolic objects with no intrinsic or utilitarian value. And yet for at least five hundred years men had been prepared to risk their lives to carry these jewels across thousands of kilometres of open sea. The necklaces moved clockwise through the years, while the arm bands flowed in reverse, always travelling in a counter-clockwise direction. Each individual involved in the trade had at least two partners, relationships that like marriages were intended to last for life, and even be inherited by subsequent generations. To one partner a voyager would give a necklace in exchange for an arm band of equal value, and to the other he would pass along an arm band and receive in return a necklace. Each contact had his second partner on another island, and thus there was a continuous distribution chain. The exchanges did not occur all at once. Once in possession of a highly valued object, one was expected to savour for a time the prestige it conferred even as one made plans ultimately to pass it along. As a single object made its way around the Kula, perhaps taking as long as twenty years to complete the passage, only to continue again, its value grew with each voyage, with each story of hardship and wonder, witchcraft and the wind, and with the names of all the great men whose lives it had passed through. Thus the sacred objects were in constant motion, encircling the scattered islands in a ring of social and magical power.

Malinowski understood and wrote of the functional purpose of the Kula ring. It established relationships over great distances among peoples of different languages, facilitating the ultimate movement back and forth of utilitarian objects, pigments and dyes, stone axes, obsidian, ceramics, polished ceremonial stones, woven goods and certain foods. The Kula also provided the context for the display of prestige and status upon which the authority of the hereditary chiefs was based. Their names were associated with the most valuable arm bands and necklaces, and it fell to them to organize and lead the voyages. Preparations were rigorous and costly. Men from widely separated villages had to be coordinated. Gardens had to be planted simply to grow the food to be consumed during the preparations for the journey. There were taboos to enforce, ritual magic to perform, feasts to celebrate, supplies to secure and store for the journey. Fleets of canoes had to be built, new sails woven from pandanus leaves, outriggers polished and painted, paddles carved and the ornate prows ritually cleansed and empowered to ward off all evil — giant sea creatures, living rocks, the witches dwelling in the deep who consumed shipwrecked men. Months went by and with each passing day the excitement grew. As Malinowski so elegantly distilled in the title of his book, the voyagers really were as Argonauts sailing forth into the unknown, in search of honour and glory, uncertain whether they would ever again see home and family, driven by the thrill of adventure and the siren call of the open water. "It is beautiful always to sail in a native canoe," Malinowski wrote his wife, Elsie. "It gives you the impression of being on a raft, quite on the surface of the water, floating as if by a miracle."

SOME YEARS AGO I was fortunate to sail through the Trobriand Islands, on a journey that began in Fiji and passed through Vanuatu and the Solomon Islands before entering the waters of Papua New Guinea. Eventually we circled much of the Kula ring, moving east to west past Woodlark Island to Kitava and Kiriwina, where Malinowski was based, and then south to the Deboyne Island group, moving as a soulava necklace in a counterclockwise direction, heading ultimately for Port Moresby. Unlike Malinowski, we travelled in considerable comfort on an expedition vessel, equipped with a small flotilla of zodiacs that allowed us to land on virtually any shore, weather and currents permitting. The place I remember most was Bodaluna Island in the Laughlin group, our first point of contact with the Kula ring. We came from the rising sun across an open expanse of ocean several hundred kilometres wide, the Solomon Sea. To the Trobriand Islanders, Bodaluna was the most extreme point of their world, an islet on a coral atoll at the easternmost limits of the Kula ring.

Bodaluna was the most remote and isolated place I had ever been, a sliver of sand on the fringe of a reef, no more than a metre above sea level at any point, and protected from the typhoons by nothing more than a scattering of coconut palms and frangipani trees. The people of the island, perhaps twenty families, drew sustenance from small gardens with soil crushed from coral, and from the reef and the sea beyond; giant clamshells littered the sand and fishnets dried along the shore. Their houses were simple structures, mostly coconut thatch on a skeleton of palm wood. The children had bronze skin, and all of them wore white and red shell necklaces and white scented blossoms in their hair.

Along the shore I came upon a Kula canoe, pulled up on the beach and protected from the elements by coconut fronds. It seemed to have been there for some time. The elegantly carved splashboard, or *lagim*, that encloses the end of the hull, and the decorative wavesplitter or *tabuya* it rests upon, were both bleached grey by the sun, and only fragments of white paint remained. I ran my fingers over the shallow carvings, all the symbols of magical wisdom and spiritual flight that had faded with exposure. It was definitely a *masawa* canoe, built expressly for the Kula, but I was surprised by how small it was, less than 2 metres wide and barely longer than the deck of the

Hokule'a was wide. Its hull caulked by tree resin, blackened with paint made from charred coconut husks and banana sap, with a short wooden mast rigged in place by fibre ropes, it lay on the sand as awkwardly as in the water, at a slight list, so that the stabilizing outrigger might just skim the surface of the sea. It was not a design that inspired confidence. Once on the water it could not come about, let alone tack into a wind. It was built to go point-to-point, sailing with the wind, like an arrow on a single trajectory. Kula implied, if nothing else, commitment.

A storm was growing to the east and the light falling through the clouds darkened great swaths of the sea, even as the western sun cast shadows on the sand and illuminated the turquoise waters immediately offshore. Out on the reef, young boys, aware of the coming storm, paddled back toward land. Looking at them, I tried to imagine what it would have been like to sit on this small island when suddenly out of the horizon emerged a fleet of Kula canoes, as many as eighty at a time, all brightly painted and decorated with cowry shells, feathers, and streamers of flowers. On board the cramped canoes some five hundred men would have been preparing for hours, anointing themselves in coconut oil and adorning their hair with red hibiscus blossoms, performing private ceremonies and casting spells conceived to seduce the islanders into giving up their Kula treasures, thus ensuring the success of the expedition. On the beach the entire population of the island, feigning hostility, would have gathered to await the summons from the leader of the visiting fleet. Still offshore, he would call out for them to be generous in their welcome, to be sure that the gifts received would be equal to those that had been carried so far and at such risk and expense. A chorus of conch trumpets from the beach would then have acknowledged the obligation, and each important man of Bodaluna would have walked into the surf bearing gifts. Only once the exchange was completed would the visitors disembark and come ashore.

How long they would stay would depend on the wind. Time meant little. Wealth was not defined as ownership, but by the prestige and status that came to one who gave well and thus secured a social network, a sort of human capital of culture, a treasury of ritual debts and obligations that would yield interest to one's clan and family forever.

As we made our way off-island, manoeuvring through the narrow channels cut by hand in the coral, I was told an amazing story. The Kula canoe I had admired belonged to a party of men who had been stranded by the wind for over four months, waiting for an opportunity to sail home. In the meantime they had worked their way quietly into the circle of life of this small coral atoll. If our ship expected to pass back this way, they had asked one of our crew, perhaps we might give them a ride. They were going east as we went west. Our ship, in fact, did expect to return, but not for a long while. Six months would be fine, had been their response. Though I do not think that this is precisely what Thor Heyerdahl had in mind, it may explain something of the courage and patience that allowed human beings to settle that impossibly vast ocean.

THREE

PEOPLES OF THE ANACONDA

"In the West, time is like gold. You save it, you lose it, you waste it, or you don't have enough of it. In the Barasana language there is no word for time." — Stephen Hugh-Jones

LET'S BEGIN THIS THIRD of the Massey Lectures with a story from the shadowy days of the Spanish Conquest. In February of 1541 Gonzalo Pizarro, half-brother of Francisco, conqueror of the Inca, began a journey across the Andes in search of El Dorado and the fabled lands of Canela, of cinnamon and gold. Leaving Quito with 220 soldiers, 4,000 native porters, and 2,000 pigs as food, the expedition crested the heights of the Cordillera and began a long, slow descent through the tangled lianas and stunted trees of the cloud forest. By the time it reached the tropical lowlands, where the riverbanks gleamed by night with black caiman, the hogs and horses had long since been consumed and most of the Indian slaves had perished, as had 140 Spaniards. The surviving men, reduced to stewing leather and wild herbs, scavenged for roots and berries that left several of them deranged by poison. In desperation Gonzalo dispatched his second-in-command, Francisco de Orellana, along with forty-nine men, down a high jungle tributary in search of provisions and deliverance. Among this group was a white-frocked Dominican friar, Gaspar de Carvajal, who wrote an astonishing account of the subsequent journey.

Reaching the Napo, just one of the 1,100 major rivers that drain the Amazon, the men led by Orellana mutinied, refusing in their agony to return upstream as per the original orders. The current was too powerful, and at any rate, no food had been found. Orellana, in a fit of legal formality, for which the Conquistadores were famous, officially resigned his commission, with Gaspar de Carvajal as his witness, that he might accept by acclamation a new command at the head of the bedraggled survivors. Abandoning Gonzalo Pizarro to his fate, Orellana and his band set off into the unknown one day after Christmas 1541, heading down the swift-flowing Napo on a launch hastily crafted from jungle trees and iron nails scavenged from the hoofs of dead horses.

Tormented by the sun, and haunted at night by the roar of howlers, the low hallucinatory drone of frogs and cicadas, and the unexpected bark of jaguars, they reached after several days the confluence of the Napo with the Río Ucayali, as the Upper Amazon is known in Peru. There, to their horror, they found the shores lined with

Indian settlements, each linked to the next by the sound of messenger drums that guaranteed a hostile reception at every bend of the river. Three Spaniards died, targets of the flying death, darts coated in curare and shot silently from the forest. Gaspar de Carvajal was himself blinded in one eye by an arrow, which fortunately for history was not poisonous. His journal records the anguish of men festering with disease, their lethargic bodies riddled with parasites, their guts wrenching from lack of food. It was cruel torment indeed, for with each passing kilometre the richness and prosperity of the native villages only increased, along with the bounty of the fields, the physical beauty and numbers of inhabitants, and the evident elaboration of high culture. After nine days and several hundred kilometres, the Spaniards entered the lands of the Omagua, and found to their astonishment a continuous series of villages reaching some 320 kilometres along the shores, each no more, as Carvajal reported, than a crossbow shot apart. One community stretched for five leagues, roughly 25 kilometres, a single concentration of thatch-roofed houses.

After six months, Orellana's group passed the confluence of the Rio Negro, a tributary four times the size of the Mississippi, that were it to exist on any other continent would be the second largest river on earth. The scale of forest, river, and sky utterly unsettled their senses. On the banks of the Rio Nhamundá, two days farther downstream, they met Indians who claimed to be vassals of a ferocious tribe of female warriors, outliers of a civilization of women who dwelt in the distant headwaters, in villages of stone at the edge of saltwater lakes. There they rode camels, wore the finest woven cloth, and worshipped the divinity of the sun in temples lined with macaw feathers and parrot plumes. To procreate they captured men solely for the purposes of breeding; all male offspring were summarily killed. A fortnight later, according to Carvajal, the expedition entered the land of the Amazons and actually encountered and did battle with squadrons of Indians led by female captains — naked women, tall and white, with long braided hair wound about the head. Each fought with the power of ten men, and it was only after several had been killed that the Spaniards, their brigantine riddled with arrows, escaped.

The farther the Spaniards drifted downstream, the more elaborate were the settlements. At the mouth of the Rio Tapajós, near the modern Brazilian town of Santarém, the expedition was met by a flotilla of two hundred war canoes, each carrying thirty men, all in full regalia, with brilliant cloaks of feathers and coronas that shone like the sun. Thousands more inhabitants stood warily along the shore. The riverbanks for a hundred kilometres were dense with houses and gardens, and away from the shore there were signs, as Carvajal wrote, of "very large cities."

When finally, on August 24, 1542, eight months after setting out on the Napo and a year and half since leaving the cool mountain air of Quito, Orellana's naked band, too weakened by hunger to row, reached salvation and the sea, they remained confounded by the wonder of the river that had brought them there. In the delta there were islands the size of European nations. The riverbanks, such as they were, lay more than 300 kilometres apart. The expedition limped out to sea and was kilometres off shore, out of sight of land, before the water turned too brackish to drink.

Returning to Peru, Gaspar de Carvajal completed his journals, a remarkable saga of adventure and discovery that was almost immediately reduced to ridicule, dismissed even by his fellow clergy as *pura mentiras*, a pack of lies. His problem lay in the fantastic story of the female warriors, which to his critics was an obvious fabrication, because it echoed so closely Greek myth and the accounts of Herodotus. The word *Amazon* is derived from "a-madzon," meaning without breast, and it had long referred to a legendary nation of women warriors living beyond the known world of the Mediterranean who reputedly sliced off their right breast to facilitate the use of the bow in battle. Such was their reputation as fighters that Hercules in his ninth labour was charged with the capture of the girdle of their queen. The discovery of such women in the savage heart of the New World was simply too much to believe, especially as Carvajal was hardly the first to have laid claim to such an encounter, albeit in a new location.

Christopher Columbus, seeking evidence of the Indies and recalling Marco Polo's discovery of an island of women in the Sea of China, described to Queen

Isabella an island of women who lived without men, wore copper armour, and took cannibals as lovers. Amerigo Vespucci found man-eating women on the Caribbean Island of Martinique. Cortés sent his cousin Francisco north along the coast of Mexico to investigate reports of a land of women ruled by a mythical black Queen Califia — hence the name California. Indeed, like El Dorado and the Fountain of Youth, the land of the women warriors was on every explorer's itinerary. In time, the European myth became modified by the fertile imagination of the Amerindian peoples, who had learned from cruel experience to tell the whites whatever it was they wanted to hear. Thus the tale of the female warriors was fed back to the Old World in a new and enlivened form, which had a ring of authenticity that transformed myth into history. King Charles V was particularly intrigued, and because of him, the river that had always been known as the Mar Dulce, the Sweet or Freshwater Sea, took a new name, the Río Amazonas, the river of the Amazons. But skeptics such as the Spanish historian Francisco López de Gómara, writing as early as 1552, remained unconvinced, dismissing Carvajal's entire account as a sensational effort to mask the fact that Orellana had committed treason in abandoning his commander, Gonzalo Pizarro, and had found on his expedition neither gold nor cinnamon, nor anything of value for the Crown. Buried by court gossip and intrigue, largely ignored by history, Carvajal's *Relación*, the record of the first European descent of the world's greatest river, would not be published until 1895. Ironically, had the friar not spoken of the Amazon women, his remarkable journal might long have been celebrated for what he undoubtedly did see and faithfully record, observations that today read as revelations to anthropologists and archaeologists. The Amazon at the time of European contact was no empty forest, but an artery of civilization and home to hundreds of thousands, indeed millions of human beings.

THE AMAZON PROVOKES CLICHÉS even as it defies hyperbole. It is, after all, the world's greatest single expanse of tropical terrestrial life, a rain forest the size of the continental United States, a blanket of biological wealth as large as the face of the full moon. Joseph Conrad described the jungle as less a forest than a primeval mob, a remnant of an ancient era when vegetation rioted and consumed the world. Travelling in the lowlands of the Putumayo in Colombia in the 1930s, the Capuchin priest Gaspar de Pinell described a sojourn in a land where "tall trees covered with growths and funereal mosses create a crypt so saddening that to the traveller it appears like walking through a tunnel of ghosts and witches." This was the Amazon as "Green Hell," the name of a popular travel account published in London in 1935. The setting is lowland Bolivia, but it could have been anywhere in the basin. On its opening page the author is blinded by the sun's glare, scorched by its rays, cowed by the eerie, creeping silence of the forest, and brought to agony "by the festering stings, the cracking drought of throat and lips, the misery of tropical rain."

By the time I became a student of botany in the 1970s, the *jungle* — a word that had long gone out of fashion — had become an Eden, but a delicate one to be sure, a "cornucopia of life," as I wrote in one of my first published papers, "far more fragile than it appears. In fact, many ecologists have called the tropical forest a counterfeit paradise. The problem is soil. In many areas, there essentially is none. It is a castle of immense biological sophistication built quite literally on a foundation of sand." This rather bold statement, as clichéd in its own way as the notion of a Green Hell, had by the time I entered graduate school become a mantra of the emerging conservation biology movement. Its scientific inspiration was a classic study by a bryologist, a student of mosses, Paul Richards, whose seminal book, *The Tropical Rainforest*, was first published in 1952.

Forests, Richards pointed out, have two major strategies for preserving the nutrient load of the ecosystem. In the temperate zone, with the periodicity of the seasons and the resultant accumulation of rich organic debris, the biological wealth is in the soil itself. In the tropics, by contrast, with constant high humidity and annual temperatures hovering around 27 degrees Celsius, bacteria and microorganisms break down the plant matter as soon as the leaves hit the forest floor. Ninety percent of the root tips may be found within the top 10 centimetres of earth. Vital nutrients are immediately recycled into the vegetation. The wealth of this ecosystem is the living forest, an exceedingly complex mosaic of thousands of interacting and interdependent living organisms.

Removing this canopy sets in motion a chain reaction of destruction. Temperatures increase dramatically, relative humidity falls, rates of evapotranspiration drop precipitously, and the mycorrhizal mats that interlace the roots of forest trees, enhancing their ability to absorb nutrients, dry up and die. With the cushion of vegetation gone, torrential rains cause erosion, which leads to further loss of nutrients and chemical changes in the soil itself. "In certain deforested areas of the Amazon," I warned ominously, "the precipitation of iron oxides in leached exposed soils has resulted in the deposition of mile upon mile of lateritic clays, a rocklike pavement of red earth in which not a weed will grow."

While fundamentally sound as a way of understanding the basic dynamics of tropical forests, this model, when applied in a sweeping manner to a region as vast as the Amazon, was as much slogan as science. For one, it implied an ecological uniformity to the basin that fifty years of field research has exposed as a gross simplification. A third of the Amazon is savannah. Perhaps half is upland forest, but there is an enormous amount of diversity not only in plant and animal species but also in geomorphology and soils. No simple scheme could possibly encompass a geographical expanse seven times the size of the province of Ontario. But the notion of fragility held for two reasons. First, it served an environmental agenda, and the very legitimate concerns that people everywhere had about the rate of deforestation in the Amazon, much of which was being caused in Brazil, in particular, by the expansion from the south of the agricultural frontier. Second, and more relevant to this story, the suggestion that the forest was a marginal environment fit Western preconceptions of what it meant to live as a native in the Amazon.

In 1743 the French explorer and geographer Charles Marie de la Condamine led the first scientific expedition to travel the length of the river. His ethnobotanical discoveries were extraordinary. He was the first to identify quinine as a treatment for malaria, to describe rubber, to examine the botanical sources of curare, and to report the existence of barbasco, the fish poisons that would yield the biodegradable insecticide rotenone. He learned about all these remarkable plants from the Indians, and yet his disdain for the peoples of the forest could not have been greater. "Before making them Christians," he wrote, "they must first be made human." He saw Indians as children, frozen in their development, trapped within a forest that he revered but of which he ultimately knew nothing.

By the time anthropologists entered the Amazon in numbers in the 1950s, the surviving indigenous cultures were for the most part living in the remote headwaters at the periphery of the basin. The main trunk of the river and the lower reaches of its principal tributaries had been settled by Europeans for more than 400 years. Indeed, a unique world had emerged, a riverine peasantry of *caboclos,* men and women of mixed heritage whose entire subsistence base was derived from indigenous antecedents and adaptations. But of the original inhabitants of the main floodplain of the Amazon, there existed only shadows in the sands, whispered messages in the forest.

Anthropologists, ethnographers in particular, naturally were drawn to the extant peoples, the "real" Indians, if you will. Many of these societies lived along the eastern flank of the Andes, in a wide arc that reached along the margin of the Amazon basin from Bolivia in the south to Colombia in the north, and then across southern Venezuela, the headwaters of the Orinoco and the southern side of the Guiana Shield. The Andes, a formidable barrier, were not traversed from the west by roads until after the Second World War. Many cultures I came to know, the Chimane and Mosetene in Bolivia, the Machiguenga and Campa in the *montaña* of Peru, the Cofán, Siona–Secoya and Atshuar in lowland Ecuador, the Yanomami in Venezuela, did not experience sustained contact until the 1960s. The Waorani, with whom I lived in 1981, were not peacefully contacted until 1958, though their homeland is scarcely 150 kilometres from Quito, the national capital of Ecuador and a city settled for well over 400 years. In 1957, five missionaries attempted to contact the Waorani and made a critical mistake. They dropped from the air eight-by-ten glossy black-and-white photographs of themselves in what we would describe as friendly gestures, forgetting that the people of the forest had never seen anything two-dimensional in their lives. The Waorani picked up the prints from the forest floor and looked behind the faces to try to find the figure. Seeing nothing, they concluded that these were calling cards from the devil, and when the missionaries arrived they promptly speared them to death. The Waorani, incidentally, did not spear only outsiders, all of whom they considered to be *cowade*, or cannibals. They speared one another. Fully 54 percent of their mortality over eight generations resulted from intra-tribal spearing raids.

The Waorani were and are an exceptional people, and their history is in many ways unique. But at the same time they fit a basic pattern shared by many of the marginal societies — marginal only in the sense that they lived literally at the margins of the basin. These cultures were for the most part small in numbers, without hierarchy or intense specialization. They tended to be acephalous, lacking overt political leaders, and perhaps most characteristically, they were endogamous. They married amongst themselves, living in isolation and often in open conflict with their neighbours. They had, of course, extraordinary gifts. Waorani hunters could smell animal urine at forty paces in the forest and identify the species. Through generations of empirical observation and experimentation, they had learned to manipulate plants with considerable skill. Poisons from plants enabled them to fish and hunt. Hallucinogenic preparations such as ayahuasca revealed levels of alchemical genius beyond the reach or understanding of science. And in making a living in the forest, they had found a way through slash-and-burn agriculture to grow food despite the nutrient-poor soils. Small plots cut from the forest were fired and burned, planted and harvested with ever-diminishing returns for perhaps three years, and then abandoned to be reclaimed by the forest. All of this activity was critically dependent on population density. Too many people would result in too many fields with no time for the vegetation to regenerate, the exhaustion of the land, and the saturation of the carrying capacity of the environment.

To a remarkable extent, this cultural scenario became the filter through which anthropologists understood indigenous life in the Amazon. Societies, it was implied, clung precariously to a perilous existence, constrained always by the environment and its limitations. In 1971, Betty Meggers, a highly regarded archaeologist at the Smithsonian Institution, published *Amazonia: Man and Culture in a Counterfeit Paradise,* a book that became required reading in virtually every introductory anthropology course on South America. Meggers depicted a world of small hunting and gathering societies, virtually unchanged in centuries, none of which could possibly have supported more than a thousand people, a figure she determined arbitrarily. Higher populations, she suggested, might have occurred on the floodplain of the lower river, as indeed Gaspar de Carvajal had reported, but evidence was vague and imprecise, and all along the main trunk of the river "the aboriginal cultural pattern had been completely destroyed within 150 years of its discovery."

But had it? Preservation of archaeological remains had been as much of a problem in the Amazon as it was in Polynesia. But beginning in the 1980s new techniques unveiled unexpected worlds. Working on the island of Marajó in the delta, archaeologists, Anna Roosevelt in particular, found evidence of a complex culture, perhaps as many as a hundred thousand people spread over thousands of square kilometres that had persisted for at least a thousand years. Near the city of Manaus at the confluence of the Rio Negro and the Amazon, massive earthen burial mounds, dating to AD 1000, provided evidence that whoever had occupied the land had exploited some 138 domesticated plants, most of which were fruit trees and palms. Botanists and ecologists, meanwhile, were discovering throughout the Amazon curious anomalies, large but isolated expanses of *terra preta,* black soil, clearly of human origins, showing that people had in fact stayed put, and actively worked to enhance the agricultural potential of the land, with charcoal for nutrient retention, organic waste as compost. William Balée, an ethnobotanist from Tulane University, suggested that as much as a tenth of the upland forests of the Amazon, an area the size of France, may have been nurtured in this manner by the original inhabitants.

These observations led other scholars to question traditional assumptions about the origins and impacts of slash-and-burn agriculture. When I lived among the Waorani, a people who still had stone tools at the time of contact, I often wondered how such an implement could possibly fell tropical hardwoods that I, as a botanist and one-time logger, could barely cut with a modern axe. Anthropologist Robert Carneiro pondered the same question and decided to experiment. To cut down a 1-metre tree with a stone axe took 115 hours, three weeks of eight-hour days. To clear a half-hectare plot took the equivalent of 153 eight-hour days. According to Betty Meggers and other authorities, such a field could only be worked intensively for three years before being abandoned. Given other demands on an individual's time — hunting, fishing, ritual obligations — it would have been totally impractical and utterly maladaptive to devote so much effort for so little return. Rather than slash, burn, plant, harvest, and move on, people would have had every incentive to stay put. Indeed, as geographer William Denevan has written, "the picture of swidden, or slash and burn, as an ancient practice by which Indians kept themselves in timeless balance with Nature is a total myth." Slash-and-burn agriculture in the Amazon may be a comparatively recent development, made possible by the post-contact introduction of steel tools. It has become over time the agricultural technology of the peripheral peoples of the basin, whose numbers are low, and whose lands have been large enough to absorb its almost grotesque inefficiencies. But clearly this was not the foundation of life among the densely populated cultures we now know to have existed along the main reaches of the Amazon.

Anthropologists today recognize that our understanding of these ancient worlds has been for too long filtered through our experience with the marginal societies that survived what was in fact a holocaust. To understand the prehistory of the basin through this lens is rather like attempting to reconstruct the history of the British Empire from the perspective of the Hebrides after London had been wiped out by a nuclear bomb. Within a century of contact, disease and slavery had swept away millions of indigenous lives. And yet, incredibly, there is one place in the Amazon where the rhythm of these great civilizations may still be felt and heard, the homeland of an extraordinary complex of cultures known collectively as the Peoples of the Anaconda.

IN 1975 WHEN I first travelled to the Northwest Amazon of Colombia I stopped en route at Villavicencio, a small city nestled into the eastern foothills of the Andes, to visit a legendary naturalist, Federico Medem, a Latvian count who had fled the Russian Revolution and found a new life in the forests of the tropical lowlands. He was an old friend of my professor at university, Richard Evans Schultes, the botanical explorer who had sparked the psychedelic movement with his discovery of the magic mushrooms in Mexico in 1938, and later spent twelve uninterrupted years in the most remote reaches of the Amazon. I found Dr. Medem in the evening at his home, a rambling compound that resembled the quarters of an old rubber trader. The house had wooden floors and a tin roof, an open veranda hung with hammocks, and walls decorated with jaguar and bushmaster skins. Overhead in his office a ceiling fan cast faint shadows across the desk as he caressed an artifact or ran his fingers over a fading map drawn by hand a century before. His most prized possession was a shaman's necklace, a single strand of palm fibre threaded through a 6-inch crystal of quartz. He described it as both the penis and crystallized semen of Father Sun, explaining that within were thirty colours, all distinct energies that had to be balanced in sacred ritual. The necklace was also the shaman's house, the place to which he went when he took yagé, the hallucinogenic potion also known as ayahuasca. Once inside, the shaman looks out at the world, over the territory of his people and the sacred sites — the forests, waterfalls, mountainous escarpments, and black water rivers — watching and watching the ways of the animals.

Long after Medem retired for the night, I remained in his office reading a book that he had recommended, *Amazonian Cosmos,* written by his good friend Gerardo Reichel-Dolmatoff, Colombia's foremost anthropologist, who was also a close colleague of Schultes. It was from Reichel that I first learned of the importance of rivers. For the Indians of the Vaupés, rivers are not just routes of communication, they are the veins of the earth, the link between the living and the dead, the paths along which the ancestors travelled at the beginning of time.

The Indians' origin myths vary but always speak of a great journey from the east, of sacred canoes brought up the Milk River from the east by enormous anacondas. Within the canoes were the first people, together with the three most important plants — coca, manioc and yagé, gifts of Father Sun. On the heads of the anaconda were blinding lights, and in the canoes sat mythical heroes in hierarchical order: chiefs; wisdom-keepers who were the dancers and chanters; warriors; shaman; and finally, in the tail, servants. All were brothers, children of the sun. When the serpents reached the centre of the world, they lay over the land, outstretched as rivers, their powerful heads forming river mouths, their tails winding away to remote headwaters, the ripples in their skin giving rise to rapids and waterfalls.

Each river welcomed a different canoe, and in each drainage the five archetypal heroes disembarked and settled, with the lowly servants heading upstream and the chiefs occupying the mouth. Thus the rivers of the Vaupés were created and populated, with the Desana people coming into being on the Río Papuri, the Barasana and Tatuyos on the upper Piraparaná, the Tucano on the Vaupés, the Makuna on the Popeyacá and lower Piraparaná, the Tanimukas and Letuama on the Miriti and Apaporis. In time, the hierarchy described in the myths broke down, and on each of the rivers the descendants of those who had journeyed in the same sacred canoe came to live together. They recognized each other as family, speakers of the same language, and to ensure that no brother married a sister, they invented strict rules. To avoid incest, a man had to choose a bride who spoke a different language.

Today, when a young woman marries, she moves to the longhouse of her husband. Their children will be raised in the language of the father but naturally will learn their mother's tongue. The mother, meanwhile, will be working with the children's aunts, the wives of their father's brothers. But each of these women may come from a different linguistic group. In a single settlement, therefore, as many as a dozen languages may be spoken, and it is quite common for an individual to be fluent in as many as five. Yet curiously, through time, there has been no corrosion of the integrity of each language. Words are never interspersed or pidginized. Nor is a language violated by those attempting to pick it up. To learn, one listens without speaking until the language is mastered.

One inevitable consequence of this unusual marriage rule — what anthropologists call linguistic exogamy — is a certain tension in the lives of the people. With the quest for potential marriage partners ongoing, and the distances between neighbouring language groups considerable, cultural mechanisms must ensure that eligible young men and women come together on a regular basis. Thus the importance, Reichel-Dolmatoff wrote, of the gatherings and great festivals that mark the seasons of the year. Through sacred dance, the recitation of myth, and the sharing of coca and yagé, these celebrations promote the spirit of reciprocity and exchange on which the entire social system depends, even as they link, through ritual, the living with their mythical ancestors and the beginning of time.

Intrigued by what I had read, I arranged passage the following morning on a military cargo flight to Mitú, a small settlement without road access perched on a bend of the Río Vaupés three hours by air from Villavicencio. There was no door on the plane, and I felt as if I were riding the back of a pickup truck through the sky. I spent the better part of a month in Mitú, botanizing with the local Indians — Cubeos and Tucanos for the most part — but never came close to the heart of their world, spiritually, culturally, or literally. The forests were so vast, the distances too great, the rivers black and stunningly beautiful but broken by an endless succession of cataracts and waterfalls.

Two years later I returned and persuaded a missionary pilot to drop me at the Catholic Mission of San Miguel on the Río Piraparaná in the homeland of the Barasana, an hour farther into the forest from Mitú. It was about as remote a destination as one could devise in the Northwest Amazon. But this too was a fleeting visit, and barriers of language and protocol — I literally dropped in from the sky unannounced, and many of the Barasana spoke little Spanish — left me with only a superficial sense of the place, and a sad feeling that with the influence of the missionaries, an extraordinary culture was destined to be lost. This was the familiar lament of anthropologists of the day. Wherever we went, we encountered what we assumed to be disappearing worlds.

But then, long after my first fumbling visits to the Northwest Amazon, something remarkable occurred. In 1986, newly elected Colombian president Virgilio Barco Vargas appointed Martin Von Hildebrand, an anthropologist and protege of Reichel-Dolmatoff, as Head of Indigenous Affairs, and told him to do something for the Indian peoples of Colombia. Martin, who had lived for years among the Tanimukas and first paddled the length of the Río Piraparaná as a young graduate student, did more than something. In five extraordinary years he secured for the Indians of the Colombian Amazon legal land rights to an area of some 250,000 square kilometres, roughly the size of the United Kingdom, establishing 162 *Resguardos* altogether — titled lands that were encoded by law in the 1991 Political Constitution of the country. Nothing like this had ever been done by a nation-state. In the years that followed, as Colombia endured the ravages of war throughout the 1990s and early days of the new century, a veil of isolation fell upon the Northwest Amazon. And behind this veil, as Martin explained when he invited me in 2006 to return with him to the Río Piraparaná, an old dream of the earth was reborn.

The night before flying out of Mitú, Martin and I huddled on the cement floor of our modest lodgings, taking coca and tobacco, as Ricardo Marin, a Barasana shaman, identified on a large map the sacred sites we were about to see from the air and visit by river and trail. Martin and his colleagues at Fundación Gaia Amazonas, a grassroots NGO working with the fifty or more ethnicities of the Colombian Amazon, had codified in two dimensions what Ricardo knew to exist in multidimensional space. In Barasana there is no word for time, and the sacred sites are not memorials or symbols of distant mythic events. They are living places, as Ricardo explained, that eternally inform the present. For his people, the past is the present, and the sacred sites are to this day inhabited by mythic beings.

The following morning our small plane rose into the clouds and then burst over the canopy like a wasp, minuscule and insignificant. The forest stretched to the horizon, with little initially to betray that people had ever set foot on the land. Ricardo sat in front of me, and I watched him intently as he took in the vista, wanting to see what he saw. We flew that morning for four hours, circumnavigating the entire world of the Peoples of the Anaconda, heading east from Mitú over the Río Papuri and then south along the Taraira and the ancient ridges that separate Colombia from Brazil. Reaching the confluence of the Río Caquetá and the Apaporis, we turned west over the great cataracts of Yuisi and Jirijirimo to the mouth of the Kananari, which we followed north across sandstone escarpments that predate the birth of the Andes. To the west I could see the distant silhouette of Cerró Campaña, small on the horizon, and the immense flat-topped ridges of Sierra de Chiribiquete, uplifted tablelands massive and impossibly remote. Clouds swept over the canopy, and at one point a perfect rainbow arched across the sky, touching the forest on both sides of the Río Apaporis, which flowed beneath it like a serpent through a silent and unchanging forest.

We landed late in the day at the dirt airstrip at San Miguel, the Catholic mission I had visited in 1977. I recognized the fields, the setting of the great longhouse, or *maloca,* and the white sands along the river where children and women bathed in the black waters of the Piraparaná. But otherwise, things seemed very different. A mission I recalled as a rather sad place of desuetude was gone. On our first night a hundred or more people gathered in the maloca, men in feather regalia, to dance, chant, and take sacred medicines, coca and tobacco, chicha and yagé. Shaman huddled over calabashes of spirit food, whispering and softly singing spells. For the first time I heard the haunting sound of the sacred yurupari trumpets, created by the ancestors at the dawn of time. Long condemned by Catholic priests as symbols of the devil, these mythic instruments had been crushed and burned during the years of the mission. That their sound was still here, inspiring new generations of Barasana, Makuna, Tatuyos, and other peoples of the river, suggested powerfully that the culture was very much alive. In the thirty years or more since my first visit, the only thing that had disappeared on the Río Piraparaná, as Martin said, were the missionaries.

Over the course of nearly a month, guided by Martin and Ricardo and other Barasana and Makuna leaders such as Maximiliano García and Reinel Ortega García, we travelled the rivers, attended ceremonies, and visited sacred sites, cataracts where culture heroes had done battle with the forces of darkness and brought order into the world, domes of black stone that held up the sky, waterfalls that ran red with the menstrual blood of Romi Kumu, the Great Mother and progenitor of the earth. Flying in to join us midway through our sojourn was Stephen Hugh-Jones, former head of anthropology at Cambridge, who with his wife Christine first lived among the Barasana in the late 1960s. He returned now as a respected elder, the only academic scholar fluent in the language. A humanist and profoundly insightful ethnographer, Stephen had dedicated much of his professional life to understanding the cosmology of the Barasana and their neighbours. His presence turned the journey into an ongoing tutorial of spirit and culture, an endless series of revelations that each day brought a deeper understanding of a subtle philosophy that was dazzling in its sophistication and profoundly hopeful in its implications.

There is no beginning and end in Barasana thought, no sense of a linear progression of time, destiny, or fate. Theirs is a fractal world in which no event has a life of its own, and any number of ideas can coexist in parallel levels of perception and meaning. Scale succumbs to intention. Every object must be understood, as Stephen told me, at various levels of analysis. A rapid is an impediment to travel but also a house of the ancestors, with both a front and a back door. A stool is not a symbol of a mountain; it is in every sense an actual mountain, upon the summit of which sits the shaman. A row of stools is the ancestral anaconda, and the patterns painted onto the wood of the stools depict both the journey of the ancestors and the striations that decorate the serpent's skin. A corona of oropendola feathers really *is* the sun, each yellow plume a ray. The infinite elements of the Barasana world spin like a carousel in the mind, and there is no one obvious point of departure for even a modest attempt to explain the profundity of the peoples' intuitions about the meaning of being alive — save perhaps the maloca, the longhouse, which is both a physical space in which the people live and a cosmic model of the entire universe.

If civilizations are measured, however crudely, by the scale of their monumental architecture — just as we measure the stonework of the Inca, the temples of the Maya — then the maloca is proof of the stunning achievements of the ancient peoples of the Amazon. These structures are enormous, their internal dimensions all-encompassing. Forty metres in length, perhaps 20 abreast, with vaulted ceilings rising to 10 metres above a dirt floor hardened by ten thousand thunderous dance steps as well as the quiet passage of children at dawn, the maloca is the womb of the kindred, the dark and cool shelter of the clan, the communal space in which occurs, and out of which emerges, every societal gesture of the spirit.

The symmetry of the structure is exquisite: eight vertical posts spaced evenly in two rows, with two smaller pairs near the doors, crossbeams, and pleated rows of thatch woven over a grid of rafters. The house posts are named for the clan ancestors. The painted designs on the front facade depict the spirit beings and the patterns of colour and visions unleashed in the mind by yagé, the sacred preparation. On a mundane level, the space is divided between the genders, with the front of longhouse being reserved for visitors and men. This is the social axis where, in the flare of resin and beeswax torches, coca is prepared at night and tobacco taken in such concentrations that sweat comes to the fingertips and the world spins wildly, yet always in harmonic resonance. The women control the opposite end of the space, where the clay griddle rests on the four corner posts of the world, and cassava, a deadly poisonous plant, is each day transformed by the mothers into food, the daily bread of the people. The sustenance emerges at one stage of its preparation from a carefully woven sieve that is itself the mouth of the anaconda.

The roof of the maloca is the sky, the house posts the stone pillars and mountains that support it. The mountains, in turn, are the petrified remains of ancestral beings, the culture heroes who created the world. The smaller posts represent the descendants of the original serpent. The ridgepole is simultaneously the path of the sun, the river of the sky, the Milky Way, the artery that separates the living from the limits of the universe. The floor is the earth, and beneath it runs the River of the Underworld, the stream of death and sorrow. Thus a celestial river crosses the sky as its inverse, a chthonic path of death, traverses the underworld. Each day the sun travels the sky from east to west, and each night it returns from west to east following the river of the underworld, which is the place of the dead. The Barasana bury their elders in the floor of the maloca, in coffins made of broken canoes. As they go about their daily lives, living within a space literally perceived as the womb of their lineage, the Indians walk above the physical remains of their ancestors. Yet inevitably, the spirits of the dead drift away, and to facilitate their departure the maloca is always built close to water. And since all rivers, including the River of the Underworld, are believed to run east, each maloca must be oriented along an east–west axis, with a door at each end, one for the men and one for the women. Thus the placement of the malocas adjacent to running streams is not just a matter of convenience. It is a way of acknowledging the cycle of life and death. The water both recalls the primordial act of creation, the river journey of the Anaconda and Mythical Heroes, and foreshadows the inevitable moment of decay and rebirth.

If the longhouse envelops the community, securing its eternal presence, celebrating its mythical origins, the earth itself is protected by a universal maloca that hovers over the land, anchored by the sacred sites. The world of the Barasana and their neighbours is as flat and round as the clay griddle the women use to make manioc bread. As clay blocks prop up the griddle, so the actual sky, the roof of the cosmic maloca, is supported by a distant ring of hills, through which pass four sacred gateways. The doors of the North and South are the Rib Doors that link the body of humanity to the cosmos. The gateway to the West is the Door of Suffering, the destiny of the dead, and the axis through which destructive forces enter and stain the world. The Water Door to the east leads to the mouth of the Milk River, the point of origin where earth fuses with sky and the sun is born. For the Barasana and Makuna, these gateways are actual places, and travelling with Ricardo Marin we saw them from the air. The world begins at the falls of Yuisi and ends at the cataract of Jirijirimo on the Río Apaporis. The hills along the Taraira, and the falls of Yurupari on the Río Vaupés and Araracuara on the Río Caquetá, the mountain escarpments beyond the Kanamari — these are all physical points of origin, a mythic geography written upon the land.

In the beginning, before the creation of seasons, before the Ancestral Mother, Romi Kumu, Woman Shaman, opened her womb, before her blood and breast milk gave rise to rivers and her ribs to the mountain ridges of the world, there was only chaos in the universe. Spirits and demons known as *He* preyed on their own kindred, bred without thought, committed incest without consequence, devoured their own young. Romi Kumu responded by destroying the world with fire and floods. Then, just as a mother turns over a warm slab of manioc bread on the griddle, she turned the inundated and charred world upside down, creating a flat and empty template from which life could emerge once again. As Woman Shaman she then gave birth to a new world: land, water, forest, and animals.

In a parallel story of creation, four great culture heroes — the Ayawa, also known as the primordial ancestors or the Thunders — came up the Milk River from the east, passing through the Water Door, pushing before them as ploughs the sacred trumpets of the Yurupari, creating valleys and waterfalls. Rivers were born of their saliva. Slivers of wood broken off by the effort gave rise to the first ritual artifacts and musical instruments. As the Ayawa journeyed toward the centre of the world, the notes of the trumpets brought into being the mountains and uplands, the posts and walls of the cosmic maloca. At every turn, the Ayawa confronted greedy demonic forces, avaricious spirits that thrived on destruction and coveted the world. Outwitting the monsters, casting them into stone, the Ayawa brought order to the universe, causing the essence and energy of the natural world to be released for the benefit of all sentient creatures and every form of life. Then, stealing the creative fire from the vagina of the Woman Shaman, they made love to her, and, fully satiated, rose into the heavens to become thunder and lightning.

Realizing that she was pregnant, Woman Shaman went downriver to the Water Door of the East, where she gave birth to the ancestral anaconda. In time the serpent retraced the harrowing journey of the Ayawa, returning in body and spirit to the riverbanks, waterfalls, and rocks, where it birthed the clan ancestors of the Barasana, Makuna, and all their neighbours. Each of these physical and geographical points of memory remains vibrant and alive, the sacred nexus where the Ayawa released to humans the raw energy of life, even as they bequeathed to all Peoples of the Anaconda the eternal obligation to manage the flow of creation.

Thus, for the people living today in the forests of the Piraparaná, the entire natural world is saturated with meaning and cosmological significance. Every rock and waterfall embodies a story. Plants and animals are but distinct physical manifestations of the same essential spiritual essence.

At the same time, everything is more than it appears, for the visible world is only one level of perception. Behind every tangible form, every plant and animal, is a shadow dimension, a place invisible to ordinary people but visible to the shaman. This is the realm of the *He* spirits, a world of deified ancestors where rocks and rivers are alive, plants and animals are human beings, sap and blood the bodily fluids of the primordial river of the anaconda. Hidden in cataracts, behind the physical veil of waterfalls, in the very centre of stones are the great malocas of the *He* spirits, where everything is beautiful — the shining feathers, the coca, the calabash of tobacco powder, which is itself the skull and brain of the sun.

It is to the realm of the *He* spirits that the shaman goes in ritual. Contrary to popular lore in the West, the shaman of the Barasana never uses or manipulates medicinal plants. His duty and sacred task is to move in the timeless realm of the *He,* embrace the primordial powers, and harness and restore the energy of all creation. He is like a modern engineer who enters the depths of a nuclear reactor to renew the entire cosmic order.

Among the Barasana, such renewal is the fundamental obligation of the living. In practice, this implies that the Barasana see the earth as potent, the forest as being alive with spiritual beings and ancestral powers. To live off the land is to embrace both its creative and destructive potential. Human beings, plants, and animals share the same cosmic origins, and in a profound sense are seen as essentially identical, responsive to the same principles, obligated by the same duties, responsible for the collective well-being of creation. There is no separation between nature and culture. Without the forest and the rivers, humans would perish. But without people, the natural world would have no order or meaning. All would be chaos. Thus the norms that drive social behaviour also define the manner in which human beings interact with the wild, the plants and animals, the multiple phenomena of the natural world, lightning and thunder, the sun and the moon, the scent of a blossom, the sour odour of death. Everything is related, everything connected, a single integrated whole. Mythology infuses land and life with meaning, encoding expectations and behaviours essential to survival in the forest, anchoring each community, every maloca, to a profound spirit of place.

These cosmological ideas have very real ecological consequences both in terms of the way people live and the impacts they have on their environment. The forest is the realm of the men, the garden the domain of women, where they give birth to both plants and children. The women cultivate thirty or more food crops and encourage the fertility and fecundity of some twenty varieties of wild fruits and nuts. The men grow only tobacco and coca, which they plant in narrow winding paths that run through the women's fields, like serpents in the grass. For the women, the act of harvesting and preparing cassava, the daily bread, is a gesture of procreation and a form of initiation. The starchy fluid left over once the grated mash has been fully rinsed is seen as female blood that can be rendered safe by heat, and drunk warm like a mother's milk. The crude manioc fibre resembles the bone of men. Fired on the griddle, shaped by female hands, the cassava is the medium through which the plant spirits of the wild are domesticated for the good of all. Like all food it has ambivalent potential. It gives life but may also bring disease and misfortune. Thus nothing can be eaten unless it has passed through the hands of an elder, and been blessed and spiritually cleansed by the shaman.

Food in this sense is power, for it represents the transfer of energy from one life form to another. As a child grows he or she is only slowly introduced to new categories of food, and severe food restrictions mark all the major passages of life — moments of initiation for a male, the first menses for a woman, transitional moments when the human being by definition is in contact with the spirit realm of the *He*. When men go to the forest to hunt or fish, it is never a trivial passage. First the shaman must travel in trance to negotiate with the masters of the animals, forging a mystical contract with the spirit guardians, an exchange based always on reciprocity. The Barasana compare it to marriage, for hunting too is a form of courtship, in which one seeks the blessing of a greater authority for the honour of taking into one's family a precious being. Meat is not the right of a hunter but a gift from the spirit world. To kill without permission is to risk death by a spirit guardian, be it in the form of a jaguar, anaconda, tapir, or harpy eagle. Man in the forest is always both predator and prey. The same cautious and established social protocols that maintain peace and respect between neighbouring clans of people, that facilitate the exchange of ritual goods, food, and women, are applied to nature. Animals are potential kin, just as the wild rivers and forests are part of the social world of people.

All of these ideas and restrictions create, as anthropologist Kaj Arhem has written, what is essentially a land management plan inspired by myth. Of the forty-five game animals available to the Barasana and Makuna, for example, only twenty are hunted with any regularity. Of some forty species of fish, perhaps twenty-five are consumed. The complex food restrictions result in a highly diversified subsistence base, which is concentrated on the lower end of the food chain. Tapir, though highly prized, is rarely hunted and is reserved at any rate for the elders. Meat in general, though important to the identity of the hunter, is far less important as a source of protein than fish or insects. Ants, larvae, and termites, along with cassava bread, are the foundations of a diet and a cuisine that is both delicious and highly sophisticated. Since virtually every bend and rapid in a river, every stream crossing and every stone is associated with a mythic event, the entire landscape is mapped in the mind of the shaman. Hunters avoid salt licks. Fishing is prohibited in places toxic with the blood of the ancestors, beaches and side channels that also happen to be spawning habitat for sabelta or palometa. Entire stretches of the Piraparaná, home to several hundred species of fish, are deemed off limits for spiritual reasons. Shamanic sanctions, though inspired by cosmology, have the very real effect of mitigating the impact of human beings on the environment. And as the mythological events that inspired such beliefs are ongoing, the consequence is a living philosophy that really does view man and nature as one.

Where this all comes alive is in ritual. Before leaving the Piraparaná, we attended a fertility ceremony in honour of Cassava Woman, an event that lasted for two days and nights, attracting hundreds of men and women and families from up and down the river to the maloca at Puerto Ortega. Our host was Reinel Ortega García, a Barasana shaman. The chief of the maloca was Patricio; his wife Rosa was Cassava Woman, symbol of fertility and continuity. All of the hierarchical leadership was in place — the chanter and the dancers, the wisdom-keeper and the chief, the shaman, and the kumu, the priest. Stephen Hugh-Jones described the roles of these distinct religious figures with a curious metaphor. The shaman, he said, is like the minister of foreign affairs; he deals laterally with the forces of nature. Meanwhile, the kumu, or priest, deals vertically, through time, with the ancestors. He does not improvise. His language, like that of the chants, is liturgical, archaic, beyond the understanding of all but those who have been taught its inner meaning. His is a canon of deep religious knowledge, and he does not deviate or improvise. To do so would be as inappropriate as a Catholic priest changing the language and prayers of the Eucharist.

Intensity of devotion was most evident in the men responsible for weaving the feathered coronas to be used in the dance. They had been isolated in the maloca for several weeks, forbidden to eat meat or fish, or to be with their wives. To create the brilliant yellow plumes they had plucked the feathers of living birds and applied a paste of frog venom and toxic berries to the breasts of the parrots, causing the new plumage, normally deep red, to emerge the colour of the sun. The regalia is not decorative. It is the literal connection to sacred space, the wings to the divine.

As the ritual begins, time collapses. There are two series of dances, separated by the liminal moments of the day, dawn, dusk, and midnight. In donning the feathers, the yellow corona of pure thought, the white egret plumes of the rain, the men become the ancestors, just as the river is the anaconda, the mountains the house posts of the world, the shaman the shape-shifter, in one moment a predator, in the next prey. He changes from fish to animal to human being and back again, transcending every form, becoming pure energy flowing among every dimension of reality, past and present, here and there, mythic and mundane. His chants recall by name every point of geography met on the ancestral journey of the Anaconda, toponyms that can be traced back with complete accuracy more than 1,600 kilometres down the Amazon to the east where the great civilizations once thrived.

White people, Ricardo told me, see with their eyes, but the Barasana see with their minds. They journey both to the dawn of time and into the future, visiting every sacred site, paying homage to every creature, as they celebrate their most profound cultural insight, the realization that animals and plants are only people in another dimension of reality. This is the essence of the Barasana philosophy. Consider for a moment what this implies, and what it tells us about the culture and its place in history. It is a tradition based on knowledge acquired through time and intense priestly study and initiation. Status accrues to the man of wisdom, not the warrior. Their malocas rival in grandeur the great architectural creations of humanity. They have a complex understanding of astronomy, solar calendars, intense notions of hierarchy and specialization. Their wealth is vested in ritual regalia as elegant as that of a medieval court. Their systems of exchange, infinitely complex, facilitate peace, not war. Their struggle to bring order to the universe, to maintain the energetic flows of life, and the specificity of their beliefs and adaptations, leaves open the very remarkable possibility that the Barasana are the survivors of a world that once existed — the complex societies and chieftains that so astonished Gaspar de Carvajal and Francisco de Orellana, the lost civilizations of the Amazon.

Perhaps, in the adaptation and cultural survival of the Barasana and Makuna and all the Peoples of the Anaconda, we can glimpse something of the beliefs and convictions that allowed untold millions to live along the banks of the world's greatest river. When the Barasana today engage in ritual and take yagé, an astonishing potion, and say that they travel through multiple dimensions, reliving the journey of the Ayawa, alighting on the sacred sites, accomplishing all of these remarkable spiritual deeds, it is because they really do. When we say that the Barasana and their neighbours both echo the ancient pre-Columbian past and point a way forward, embodying a model of how human societies can live and thrive in the Amazon basin without laying waste to the forests, it is because they really can.

FOUR

SACRED GEOGRAPHY

"The intuitive mind is a sacred gift and the rational mind is a faithful servant. We have created a society that honours the servant and has forgotten the gift."
— Albert Einstein

IN A RUGGED KNOT OF mountains in the remote reaches of northern British Columbia lies a stunningly beautiful valley known to the First Nations as the Sacred Headwaters. There, on the southern edge of the Spatsizi Wilderness, the Serengeti of Canada, are born in remarkably close proximity three of Canada's most important salmon rivers, the Stikine, the Skeena, and the Nass. In a long day, perhaps two, it is possible to walk through open meadows, following the tracks of grizzly, caribou, and wolf, and drink from the very sources of the three rivers that inspired so many of the great cultures of the Pacific Northwest, the Gitxsan and Wet'suwet'en, the

Carrier and Sekani, the Tsimshian, Nisga'a, Tahltan, Haisla, and Tlingit. Keep on for another three days and you'll reach the origins of the Finlay, headwaters of the Mackenzie, Canada's greatest river of all.

The only other place I know where such a wonder of geography occurs is in Tibet, where from the base of Mount Kailash arise three of the great rivers of Asia, the Indus, Ganges, and Brahmaputra, vital arteries that bring life to more than a billion people downstream. Revered by Hindu, Buddhist, and Jain, Kailash is considered so sacred that no one is allowed to walk upon its slopes, let alone climb to its summit. The thought of violating its flanks with industrial development would represent for all peoples of Asia an act of desecration beyond all imaginings. Anyone who would even dare propose such a deed would face the most severe sanctions, in both this world and the next.

In Canada, we treat the land quite differently. Against the wishes of all First Nations, the government of British Columbia has opened the Sacred Headwaters to industrial development. These are not trivial initiatives. Imperial Metals Corporation proposes an open-pit copper and gold mine processing 30,000 tons of ore a day from the flank of Todagin Mountain, home to one of the largest populations of Stone sheep in the world. Its tailings pond, if constructed, would drain directly into the headwater lake chain of the Iskut River, the principal tributary of the Stikine. Over its lifetime of twenty-five years, the mine would generate 183 million tons of toxic tailings and 307 million tons of waste rock, which would need to be treated for acid drainage for over 200 years. Two other mining concerns, Fortune Minerals Limited and West Hawk Development Corp., would tear into the headwater valley itself, on a similar scale, with open-pit anthracite coal operations that would level entire mountains.

The largest project is a proposal by Royal Dutch Shell to extract coalbed methane (CBM) gas from the same anthracite deposit, across an enormous tract of more than 4,000 square kilometres. Should this development go ahead it would imply a network of several thousand wells, linked by roads and pipelines, laid upon the landscape of the entire Sacred Headwaters basin. CBM recovery is by all accounts a highly invasive process. To free methane from anthracite, technicians must fracture the coal seams with massive injections of chemical agents under high pressure, more than a million litres at a shot, a technique that in some deposits liberates enormous volumes of highly toxic water. More than 900 different chemicals, many of them powerful carcinogens, are registered for use, but for proprietary reasons companies do not have to disclose the identity of the solutions employed at any given site.

Environmental concerns aside, think for a moment of what these proposals imply about our culture. We accept it as normal that people who have never been on the land, who have no history or connection to the country, may legally secure the right to come in and by the very nature of their enterprises leave in their wake a cultural and physical landscape utterly transformed and desecrated. What's more, in granting such mining concessions, often initially for trivial sums to speculators from distant cities, companies cobbled together with less history than my dog, we place no cultural or market value on the land itself. The cost of destroying a natural asset, or its inherent worth if left intact, has no metric in the economic calculations that support the industrialization of the wild. No company has to compensate the public for what it does to the commons, the forests, mountains, and rivers, which by definition belong to everyone. As long as there is a promise of revenue flows and employment, it merely requires permission to proceed. We take this as a given for it is the foundation of our system, the way commerce extracts value and profit in a resource-driven economy. But if you think about it, especially from the perspective of so many other cultures, touched and inspired by quite different visions of life and land, it appears to be very odd and highly anomalous human behaviour.

In this, the fourth of the Massey Lectures, I would like to reflect on this particular attitude of ours, this manner in which we have reduced our planet to a commodity, a raw resource to be consumed at our whim. In doing so, I will suggest rather hopefully that, as the anthropological lens reveals, there are in fact many other options, any number of different ways of orienting ourselves in place and landscape. The multiple ways in which people all over the world settle themselves in geographical and ecological space reflect, as Father Thomas Berry has so beautifully written, the infinite and the impossible, the innocent and the profane, the sacred and the sordid, all of which represent unique dreams of the earth.

During the Renaissance and well into the Enlightenment, in our quest for personal freedom, we in the European tradition liberated the human mind from the tyranny of absolute faith, even as we freed the individual from the collective, which was the sociological equivalent of splitting the atom. And, in doing so, we also abandoned many of our intuitions for myth, magic, mysticism, and, perhaps most importantly, metaphor. The universe, declared René Descartes in the seventeenth century, was composed only of "mind and mechanism." With a single phrase, all sentient creatures aside from human beings were devitalized, as was the earth itself. "Science," as Saul Bellow wrote, "made a housecleaning of belief." Phenomena that could not be positively observed and measured could not exist. By the nineteenth century the positivist tradition defined even the study of society, with the invention of the social sciences, an oxymoronic turn of phrase if ever there was one. The triumph of secular materialism became the conceit of modernity. The notion that land could have anima, that the flight of a hawk might have meaning, that beliefs of the spirit could have true resonance, was ridiculed, dismissed as ridiculous.

For several centuries the rational mind has been ascendant, even though science, its finest expression, can still in all its brilliance only answer the question *how*, but never come close to addressing the ultimate question: *why*. The inherent limitation of the scientific model has long provoked a certain existential dilemma, familiar to many of us taught since childhood that the universe can only be understood as the random action of minute atomic particles spinning and interacting in space. But more significantly, the reduction of the world to a mechanism, with nature but an obstacle to overcome, a resource to be exploited, has in good measure determined the manner in which our cultural tradition has blindly interacted with the living planet.

As a young man I was raised on the coast of British Columbia to believe that the rainforests existed to be cut. This was the essence of the ideology of scientific forestry that I studied in school and practised in the woods as a logger. The rotation cycle — the rate at which forests were to be felled across the province, and thus the foundation of sustained yield forestry — was based on the assumption that all of the old growth would be cut and replaced with tree farms. The very language of the academic discipline of forestry was disingenuous, as if conceived to mislead. The "annual allowable cut" was not a limit never to be exceeded but a quota to be met. The "falldown effect," the planned decline in timber production as the old growth was depleted, was promoted as if it were a natural phenomenon when it was, as everyone in the logging camps acknowledged, a stunning admission that the forests had been drastically overcut every year since modern forestry was implemented in the 1940s. "Multiple-use forestry," which implied that forests were to be managed for a variety of purposes, began with a clear-cut. Old growth was harvested, though it was never planted and no one expected it to grow back. Ancient forests were described as "decadent" and "overmature" when by any ecological definition they were at their richest and most biologically diverse stage. The intrinsic value of these rare and remarkable rainforests, like the inherent worth of the mountains and meadows of the Sacred Headwaters, had no place in the calculus of the planning process.

This cultural perspective was profoundly different from that of the First Nations, those living on Vancouver Island at the time of European contact, and those still there. If I was sent into the forest to cut it down, a Kwakwaka'wakw youth of similar age was traditionally dispatched during his Hamatsa initiation into those same forests to confront Huxwhukw and the Crooked Beak of Heaven, cannibal spirits living at the north end of the world, all with the goal of returning triumphant to the potlatch that his individual spiritual discipline and fortitude might revitalize his entire people with the energy of the wild. The point is not to ask or suggest which perspective is right or wrong. Is the forest mere cellulose and board feet? Was it truly the domain of the spirits? Is a mountain a sacred place? Does a river really follow the ancestral path of an anaconda? Who is to say? Ultimately these are not the important questions.

What matters is the potency of a belief, the manner in which a conviction plays out in the day-to-day lives of a people, for in a very real sense this determines the ecological footprint of a culture, the impact that any society has on its environment. A child raised to believe that a mountain is the abode of a protective spirit will be a profoundly different human being from a youth brought up to believe that a mountain is an inert mass of rock ready to be mined. A Kwakwaka'wakw boy raised to revere the coastal forests as the realm of the divine will be a different person from a Canadian child taught to believe that such forests are destined to be logged. The full measure of a culture embraces both the actions of a people and the quality of their aspirations, the nature of the metaphors that propel them onward.

Herein, perhaps, lies the essence of the relationship between many indigenous peoples and the natural world. Life in the malarial swamps of New Guinea, the chill winds of Tibet, the white heat of the Sahara, leaves little room for sentiment. Nostalgia is not a trait commonly associated with the Inuit. Nomadic hunters and gatherers in Borneo have no conscious sense of stewardship for mountain forests that they lack the technical capacity to destroy. What these cultures have done, however, is to forge through time and ritual a relationship to the earth that is based not only on deep attachment to the land but also on far more subtle intuition — the idea that the land itself is breathed into being by human consciousness. Mountains, rivers, and forests are not perceived as being inanimate, as mere props on a stage upon which the human drama unfolds. For these societies, the land is alive, a dynamic force to be embraced and transformed by the human imagination. This sense of belonging and connection is nowhere more perfectly elaborated than along the spine of the Andean Cordillera of South America and in the heights of the Sierra Nevada de Santa Marta, an isolated massif that soars to about 6,000 metres above the Caribbean coastal plain of Colombia. And it finds perhaps its most abstract and consequential expression in the exquisitely subtle philosophy of the Aboriginal peoples of Australia. These are the places I would like to explore in this lecture.

I FIRST TRAVELLED SOUTH through the Andes in the spring of 1974, when as a young student I was fortunate to join a botanical expedition charged with the task of unravelling the mysteries of a plant known to the Inca as the Divine Leaf of Immortality – coca, the notorious source of cocaine. It was a remarkable assignment. Cocaine, first isolated from the leaf in 1855, had revolutionized modern medicine, particularly ophthalmology, by allowing for the painless removal of cataracts. It remains our most powerful topical anaesthetic. The essences of the leaves still contribute to the flavour of one of the world's most popular drinks: coca makes Coca-Cola "the real thing." The soft drink company in turn provides the pharmaceutical industry with all the legal cocaine employed today by the medical profession.

By the mid-1970s the Latin American cartels were emerging, though no one knew quite how, and no one realized how sordid and murderous they would become. The illicit trade, such as it was, still lay in the hands of the independent drifter. Efforts to eradicate the traditional fields had been underway for half a century, but these misguided purges had nothing to do with cocaine and everything to do with the cultural identity of those who revered the plant. Physicians in Lima, in particular, whose concern for the indigenous peoples of the Andes was matched in its intensity only by their ignorance of Indian life, glanced up to the Sierra in the 1920s and saw dreadful poverty, poor sanitation and nutrition, high rates of illiteracy, infant mortality, and disease. They sought an explanation. The real issues of land distribution, economic exploitation, and the persistence of debt peonage challenged the foundations of their own class structure, so they settled upon coca as the culprit. Every conceivable social ill and pathology was blamed on the plant. The eradication of the traditional fields became a state priority, and with the intervention of the United Nations in the late 1940s, international policy.

Remarkably, despite this public concern and hysteria, in 1974 little was known scientifically about the plant. The botanical origins of the domesticated species, the chemistry of the leaf, the pharmacology of coca chewing, the plant's role in nutrition, the geographical range of the cultivated varieties, the relationship between the wild and cultivated species — all these remained mysteries. It was widely acknowledged, of course, that coca was revered in the Andes as no other plant. In the time of the

Inca no holy shrine could be approached if the supplicant did not have coca in the mouth. Unable to cultivate it at the elevation of the imperial capital of Cusco, the Inca replicated the plant in gold and silver, in ritual fields that coloured the landscape. To this day no significant event occurs in the highlands without a reciprocal exchange of the energy of the leaf with the essence of Pachamama, the feminine earth essence. No field can be planted or harvested, no child brought into the world, no elder led into the realm of the dead without the mediation of the sacred plant.

To the dismay of certain elements in the U.S. government, our team conducted the first nutritional study of the plant in 1975, and what was discovered proved to be astonishing. The plant had a small amount of the alkaloid, roughly 0.5 to 1 percent dry weight, a modest concentration that was benignly absorbed through the mucous membrane of the cheek. But it also contained a considerable range of vitamins, and more calcium than any plant ever studied by the U.S. Department of Agriculture, which made it ideal for a diet that traditionally lacked a dairy product. It was also suggested that the leaves produced enzymes that enhanced the body's ability to digest carbohydrates at high elevation, ideal for the potato-based diet of the Andes. This scientific revelation put into stark relief the draconian efforts that are underway to this day to eradicate the traditional fields. Coca was not a drug, but a sacred food that had been used benignly by the people of the Andes as a mild stimulant without any evidence of toxicity, let alone addiction, for more than 4,000 years.

With coca as my lens, the richness of the contemporary pan-Andean world came slowly into focus. The arrival in Peru of the Spaniards in the sixteenth century unleashed a cataclysm, but out of that terrible encounter emerged a remarkable cultural amalgam that to this day draws inspiration from both Christianity and ancient pre-Columbian beliefs. The conquistadors did everything in their power to crush the spirit of the Andes, destroying all religious temples and icons. But every time the Spaniards planted a cross or built a church on top of a demolished shrine they simply affirmed in the eyes of the people the inherent sacredness of the place. For it was not a building that the Indians worshipped, it was the land itself: the rivers and waterfalls, the rocky outcrops and mountain peaks, the rainbows and stars. Five hundred years of European domination, with all manner of injustices, has failed to quell the essential impulse of the Andes, which is still felt in every hamlet and mountain glen, among the tussock grasses of the *puna* where alpaca and vicuña graze, and along the stone-lined streets of every city and crossroads of the long-lost empire.

Between southern Colombia and Bolivia there are today 6 million people who speak Quechua, the language of the Inca, as their mother tongue. They are for the most part farmers, and their gifts to the world have included the potato and tomato, tobacco, maize, quinine, and coca. To them, the land is literally alive.

The mountains are mystical beings that gather the rain, create weather, bring fertility to the soil and abundance to the fields, or in their wrath sow destruction and chaos, unleashing deadly storms or frosts that can destroy in mere moments the work of a year, as occurred in 1983 when hail in fifteen minutes wiped out the entire corn crop of the vast Cusco region.

Every community in the southern Andes is still dominated by a specific protective mountain deity, an *Apu* that directs the destiny of those born in its shadow. Thus with each step the people even today walk through a landscape they believe to be sacred. Just as the traditional agricultural economy remains based on the exchange of labour, so too reciprocity defines the connection between the community and the land, ritual obligations and relationships never spoken about and never forgotten. Pachamama and the apus will nurture a people, as long as they in turn are treated with proper care and reverence.

When men and women meet on a trail, they pause and exchange *k'intus* of coca, three perfect leaves aligned to form a cross. Turning to face the nearest apu they bring the leaves to their mouths and blow softly, a ritual invocation that sends the essence of the plant back to the earth, the community, the sacred places, and the souls of the ancestors. The exchange of leaves is a social gesture, a way of acknowledging a human connection. But the blowing of the *phukuy*, as it is called, is an act of spiritual reciprocity, for in giving selflessly to the earth, the individual ensures that in time the energy of the coca will return full circle, as surely as rain falling on a field will inevitably be reborn as a cloud. This subtlety of gesture, in its own way a prayer, is celebrated on a grand scale in annual community-based rituals of commitment and engagement.

Much of what I know of the Andes I learned in Chinchero, a stunningly beautiful valley just outside of Cusco. The town centre rests upon the ruins of the summer palace of Topa Inca Yupanqui, second of the great Incan rulers. Exquisite terraces fall away to an emerald plain, the floor of an ancient seabed that rises in the north to the distant peaks of the Vilcabamba, the last redoubt of the empire. To the east, the undulating slopes of Antakillqa, the sacred Apu, dominate the skyline. Perched at the height of the ruins is the colonial church where, in 1981, I stood as godfather for a lovely baby boy, Armando, sealing a friendship with his family that prospers to this day.

Once each year in Chinchero, at the height of the rainy season, a remarkable event occurs: the *mujonomiento,* the annual running of the boundaries. The fastest boy in each hamlet is given for one day the honour of becoming a transvestite, a *waylaka*. Dressed in the clothing of sisters or mothers, and carrying white ritual banners, the waylakas must lead all able-bodied men on a run. The distance travelled is only 30 kilometres, but the route crosses two soaring Andean ridges. The run begins at 3,500 metres in the village plaza, drops 300 metres through the ruins to the base of Antakillqa, and then ascends about 900 metres to the summit spur before falling away to the valley on the far side, only to climb once more to reach the grasslands of the divide and the long trail home. It is a race but also a pilgrimage, for the boundaries are marked by mounds of earth, holy sites where prayers are uttered, coca is given to the earth, libations of alcohol to the wind, and the waylaka must dance, spinning in a rhythmic vortex that draws to the sacred peaks the feminine essence and the energy of the women left behind in the villages far below. With each ritual gesture the runners lay claim to the earth. This is the essential metaphor. One enters the day as an individual, but through exhaustion and *sacrifice*, a word derived from the Latin "to make sacred," one emerges fused to the pulse of a single community that has through ritual devotion proclaimed its sense of belonging and secured its place in sacred geography.

Pilgrimage, movement through landscape to the shadow of the divine, has been a central feature of Andean life since the beginning of memory. To make offerings, Incan priests climbed to mountain summits of 6,500 metres, heights that would not be achieved in the European tradition for 400 years. In the wake of the Conquest these pilgrimages continued, taking on new resonance and forms with the infusion of Christianity, but always remaining rooted in ancient notions of landscape and mystical power. Localized celebrations such as that of the mujonomiento in Chinchero contain the same thematic elements encountered in the great pan-Andean pilgrimages that even today draw tens of thousands of people from communities all over the southern Andes.

A year or so after first running the boundaries with the waylakas, I travelled with my good friend Nilda Callanaupa and a large contingent from Chinchero to the sacred valley of the Sinakara, site of the Qoyllur Rit'i Festival, the Star Snow Festival, perhaps the most arduous and spiritually illuminating of all Andean pilgrimages. Located some 130 kilometres due east of Cusco, six hours by road to the trailhead, the destination is a high natural amphitheatre, a verdant basin located at some 4,750 metres, dominated by the three tongues of the Colquepunku glacier fronting the valley like an altar. According to Catholic belief, a miracle occurred in the Sinakara in the late eighteenth century when a young boy saw a dazzling apparition of Christ. A shrine was built upon the site, and the image of the Lord may still be seen in the stone.

For the Inca, this rock was already sacred, as was the entire valley. To them, matter was fluid. Bones were not death but life crystallized, and thus potent sources of energy, like a stone charged by lightning or a plant brought into being by the sun. Water is vapour, but in its purest form it is ice, the shape of snowfields on the flanks of mountains, the glaciers that are the highest and most sacred destination of the pilgrims. The mountains are known as the *Tayakuna,* the fathers, and some are so powerful that it can be dangerous even to look at them. Other sacred places, such as a cave or a mountain pass or a waterfall where the rushing water speaks as an oracle, are honoured as the *Tirakuna*. These are not spirits dwelling within landmarks. Rather, the reverence is for the actual places themselves. The rivers are the open veins of the earth, the Milky Way their heavenly counterpart. Rainbows are double-headed serpents that emerge from hallowed springs, arch across the sky, and bury themselves again in the earth. Shooting stars are bolts of silver. Behind them lie all the heavens, including the dark patches of cosmic dust, the negative constellations, which to the people of the highlands are as meaningful as the clusters of stars that form animals in the sky.

The Inca considered Cusco to be the navel of the world. The Temple of the Sun, the Coricancha, was the axis from which radiated, to all points on the horizon, forty-one conceptual lines, their alignments determined by the rise and fall of the stars and constellations, the sun and the moon. Along these sightlines, or *ceques*, were hundreds of sacred sites, each with its own day of celebration, each revered and protected by a specific community. In this way each person and every clan, though rooted to a specific locality, was bound to the cosmological framework of the empire. These shrines, or *huacas* — like the sacred stone of the Sinakara where Christ miraculously and somewhat conveniently appeared just two years after the Spaniards suppressed the last great revolt of the Inca — were stations on holy paths that existed in both a literal and metaphysical sense. During times of great significance, the summer solstice or the passing of an Inca, the priests would call for sacrifices. The chosen, children and animals blessed by the Sun, were called to Cusco from all parts of the empire. Some were killed in the capital; others were selected to carry portions of the sacrificial blood back to their communities, where in due course they too would be killed. The entourages arrived in Cusco by road, but on leaving they followed the sacred routes of the ceques, walking in a straight direction over mountains and across rivers, sometimes for hundreds of kilometres, visiting local shrines, paying homage to the perfection of their fate. These journeys, as much as the sacrifice of the children, realigned the people with the Inca and represented symbolically the triumph of empire over the imposing landscape of the Andes.

Located due east of Cusco, the Sinakara Valley is charged with metaphysical power. It opens to the west to the flank of Ausangate, the most important of all Apus. Aligned with Cusco in cosmological space and time by the ceque lines, it also marks the border between two of the four quadrants of the empire, known as "Tawantinsuyu," the Four Quarters of the World. To the south and east is Collasuyo, embracing the altiplano of Bolivia, Titicaca, and all the mountains of the Sun. North and east is Antisuyo, the cloud forests and tropical lowlands, the one known part of their world never fully conquered by the Inca. Thus the central opposition in Incan cosmology and thought, upper and lower, mountain and forest, civilized and savage, is played out in ritual when the pilgrims arrive at the Sinakara from all points of the horizons to honour the Lord of Qoyllur Rit'i.

For most of the year the Sinakara Valley and the sanctuary lie still and alone, visited only by the odd shepherd. But for three days between the movable feasts of the Ascension and Corpus Christi, as the Pleiades, the Seven Sisters, re-emerge in the night sky, generally in the first days of June, as many as 40,000 pilgrims converge at the base of the mountain, some arriving on foot, some by mule, and others in open trucks and buses. From the small village at the end of the road, the narrow traffic of pilgrims slowly makes its way up a trail that climbs steadily for nine kilometres, a route that is marked by stone altars and cairns, the stations of the cross, where men and women pause to pray and make offerings. Each carries a bundle of small stones, a symbolic burden of sin to be lightened one by one as the valley comes near. Above the skyline to the west hovers the summit of Ausangate. All the communities of the southern Andes are represented, jungle dancers from Paucartambo, groups from Puno and Titicaca, the plains of Anta, Cusco, and the Sacred Valley of the Urubamba. Mules and donkeys carry food and supplies; all people must walk, even the crippled, who drag their broken bodies up the trail, inch by inch, foot by foot.

At 4,750 metres the air is cold even with a bright sun, yet the Sinakara, reached after several hours, feels warm from the presence of so many devotees. The atmosphere is festive and profound, a pageant of colour, prayer, dance, and song. Ritual banners and flags decorate the hillsides, which appear to vibrate in the wind. Along the valley floor each community stakes its ground, and blankets and ponchos of a dozen hues form a quilt that spreads on both sides of the small stream that nourishes everyone. Jungle warriors, or *chunchus,* wear headdresses festooned with parrot feathers and tunics dyed crimson with *cochineal.* The mountains are embodied in the *pablitos,* or *ukukus,* masked men from all the highland communities, hundreds of tricksters dressed as bears and charged with keeping the peace, controlling the crowds and performing the most essential of all the rituals. These symbolic embodiments of mountain and jungle meet in mock struggles, theatre set pieces that recall ancient battles, real and imagined, and the constant tension between the two oppositional poles of Andean existence. As the men dance and bluff, pose and posture, the women gather inside the sanctuary, which glows with the light of thousands of candles, many the height of a tall child. At dusk, a pall of smoke hovers over the meadows. There is a constant cacophony of brass bands, flutes, harps, and drums, the high falsetto voices of the dancers, and the explosion of fireworks. For three days and nights no one sleeps. The very ground shakes with the movement of the dancers and the slow throbbing tone of the ritual processions.

Beneath the gaiety and devotion, there is an intensely serious purpose to the ritual. Mountain deities can be wrathful or beneficent. Ice and snow are both a source of power and a miasma of disease. The glaciers are fearful domains, not because of any physical danger, though pilgrims do die of cold and exposure each year, but because they are the abode of the *condenados*, souls cursed until the end of time. According to Incan mythology the ukuku is the offspring of a woman and a bear, a supernatural creature uniquely empowered to confront and defeat the condenados. Thus it falls upon them, with their high-pitched cries and masked faces, to perform the most dangerous and solemn act of the Qoyllur Rit'i. Like Christ himself they must bear the burdens of the cross. As processions of pilgrims carry the statues of saints through the valley, the ukukus after a moonlight vigil lift the crosses from their village churches and carry them 800 metres up the flanks of Colquepunku, where they implant them in the glaciers to be charged by the energy of the mountain and the earth. Then, before dawn on the morning of the third day, roped together by whips, they climb back to the ice to retrieve the crosses as, far below, thousands of pilgrims kneel in silent prayer. All eyes are on the summit, in homage to the apus.

To the west, Ausangate is the first mountain to glow with the rays of dawn. The light moves slowly down its flanks and gradually fills the lower valleys. Once the sun comes up, the crosses come down and make their way on the backs of ukukus through the Sinakara and out through the pass, into the trucks that will bring them back to the villages. The men also carry from the mountain blocks of ice, which in a sense completes the devotional cycle: The people go to the heights of the mountain to make prayers and pay homage to the divine. In the form of ice, the essence of the mountain returns to the valley to bring life, fertility to the fields, well-being to the families, and health to the animals. It is a living dynamic relationship between people, the mountains, and the gods, a reciprocal trinity of trust and renewal, a collective prayer for the cultural survival of the entire pan-Andean world.

The vitality and authority of the Qoyllur Rit'i Festival, the symbolic resonance and meaning of its rituals, the lessons it conveys to the young anticipate a hopeful future even as they provoke a more profound understanding of the past and the legacy of the Inca.

When I returned to Cusco from the Sinakara, I joined another friend, Johan Reinhard, godfather of my youngest daughter, on a journey down the sacred valley to visit Machu Picchu. A mountaineer and high-altitude archaeologist, Johan has climbed some 200 Andean peaks of 5,000 metres or higher, searching for evidence of pre-Columbian ritual burials and sacrifices. He made history in 1995 when, near the summit of Ampato at an elevation where most people can barely breathe, he uncovered the "Ice Maiden," the perfectly preserved mummified remains of a young girl sacrificed some 500 years ago. Johan, more than anyone I know, understands the relationship in the Andes between land and culture through time. When he comes upon a ruin for the first time, his eyes go immediately to the skyline and the sacred peaks. By seeking clues in geography, in the orientation of mountains and rivers, in the movement of celestial bodies, in the configuration of the archaeology of tomorrow in the landscape of today, he was able to solve the mystery of the most legendary archaeological site in South America.

When in 1911 Hiram Bingham discovered Machu Picchu, he famously described it as a "Lost City." In truth, the complex was always an integral part of the Incan Empire, clearly linked to the network of roads that reached back to Cusco and extended for 40,000 kilometres, binding together the longest empire ever forged in the Americas. Situated on a strategic spur high above the Urubamba River, Machu Picchu was perfectly positioned to guard the approaches to the Sacred Valley while at the same time dominating the eastern lowlands of Antisuyo, the source of coca, medicinal plants, and shamanic inspiration. It was a ritual centre, certainly, established as the royal estate of Pachacuti, the first of the three great Incan rulers who forged an empire that endured for less than a century. Studies of the canals and waterways leave little doubt that Machu Picchu was built from a single architectural plan that was itself conceived, as Johan determined, within the framework of Incan cosmology, and rooted in ancient Andean notions of sacred geography. Those who designed the complex climbed every surrounding peak and built high survey platforms to observe by day and night the position of mountains and the movement of constellations. Theirs was not a simple task of engineering. The mountain deities influenced and inspired every aspect of Incan life from the fertility of the soil and the predictability of the rains to the success of armies and the well-being and fecundity of the Sun King and his sister Queen.

The two most sacred mountains of the Inca were Ausangate, as we have seen, overlooking the valley of the Qoyllur Rit'i, and Salcantay, due south of Machu Picchu. The actual Apu of Machu Picchu is Huayna Picchu, the iconic sugarloaf peak that dominates the site. The sacred centre of Machu Picchu is the Intihuatana, a curious carved stone that Bingham called the "Hitching Post of the Sun." Johan was the first to notice that the Intihuatana echoed the shape of Huayna Picchu, and that the play of light on the stone throughout the day also replicated the ebb and flow of shadows on Huayna Picchu. Just a few steps to the south of the Intihuatana, a low altar is carved in stone. At the summit of Huayna Picchu is a twin altar of identical shape. A direct north-south bearing from the summit, Johan observed, bisected the Intihuatana and the two altars, and continued south to pierce the heart of Salcantay, the major peak of the entire region. Huayna Picchu, the Intihuatana, and Salcantay were configured in a perfect north-south alignment. When the Southern Cross rises to its highest point in the sky, it sits directly over the summit of Salcantay. The Southern Cross, enveloped by the Milky Way, was one of the most important constellations of the Inca. This revelation brought Johan's attention back to the Urubamba River, which to the Inca was the earthly equivalent of the Milky Way. Like a serpent, the Urubamba coils around Machu Picchu as it falls away to the Amazon. In myth, it was the avenue along which Viracocha walked at the dawn of time when he brought the universe into being.

But where is the Urubamba born? On the flanks of Ausangate, which dominates today the site of the Qoyllur Rit'i. Just as the melting snows of Salcantay brought life to Machu Picchu, so the ice and snows of the glaciers overlooking the Sinakara bring inspiration to the people of the Andes today. Five hundred years after the Spanish Conquest, these ancient notions of sacred geography continue to define and nurture social existence, to link the living with the dead, the past with the future, just as they did in the time of the Inca.

IF IN THE SOUTHERN ANDES these original intuitions may be sensed in ritual, distilled from the crucible of five centuries of Christian influence and domination, there is one place in South America where the pre-Columbian voice remains direct and pure, unfettered by any filter save the slow turning of the world. In a bloodstained continent, the Indians of the Sierra Nevada de Santa Marta were never fully vanquished by the Spaniards. Descendants of an ancient civilization called the Tairona and numbering perhaps 30,000 today, the Kogi, Arhuacos, and Wiwa long ago escaped death and pestilence to settle in a mountain paradise that soars 6,000 metres above the Caribbean coastal plain of Colombia.

There, over the course of 500 years, they were inspired by an utterly new dream of the earth, a revelation that affirmed the existence of eternal laws that balanced the baroque potential of the human mind and spirit with all the forces of nature. The three peoples, separated by language but closely related by myth and memory, share a common adaptation and the same fundamental religious convictions. To this day they remain true to their ancient laws — the moral, ecological, and spiritual dictates of the Serankua and the Great Mother — and are still led and inspired by a ritual priesthood of *mamos*. They believe and acknowledge explicitly that they are the guardians of the world, that their rituals maintain the balance and fertility of life. They are fully aware that their common ancestors, the Tairona, in 1591 waged fierce but futile war against the invaders. In their mountain redoubt, lost to history for at least three centuries, they chose deliberately to transform their civilization into a devotional culture of peace.

When the mamos (or priests) speak, they instantly reveal that their reference points are not of our world. They refer to Columbus as if his arrival were a recent event. They talk of the Great Mother as if she were alive — and for them she is, resonant and manifest in every instant in their concept of *aluna,* a word that translates as water, earth, matter, generative spirit, life force. What is important, what has ultimate value, what gives life purpose is not what is measured and seen but what exists in the realm of aluna, the abstract dimension of meaning.

The nine-layered universe, the nine-tiered temple, the nine months a child spends in its mother's womb are all reflections of divine creation, and each informs the others. Thus a *liana* is also a snake, the mountains a model of the cosmos. The conical hats worn by Arhuaco men represent the snowfields of the sacred peaks. The hairs on a person's body echo the forest trees that cover the mountain flanks. Every element of nature is imbued with higher significance, such that even the most modest of creatures can be seen as a teacher, and the smallest grain of sand is a mirror of the universe.

In this cosmic scheme people are vital, for it is only through the human heart and imagination that the Great Mother may become manifest. For the Indians of the Sierra Nevada, people are not the problem but the solution. They call themselves the Elder Brothers and consider their mountains to be the "heart of the world." We outsiders who threaten the earth through our ignorance of the sacred law are dismissed as the Younger Brothers.

In many ways the homeland of the Kogi, Arhuacos, and Wiwa is indeed a microcosm of the world and thus metaphorically its symbolic heart. The Sierra Nevada de Santa Marta is the highest coastal mountain formation on earth. Geologically unconnected to the Andes, which form the Colombian frontier with Venezuela to the east, it floats as its own tectonic plate, triangular in outline, 150 kilometres to each side, attached to the South American continent but separated from it by rift valleys on all sides. Drained by thirty-five major watersheds, with a total area of more than 20,000 square kilometres, the massif rises within 50 kilometres from sea to summit ice. Within its undulating folds and deep valleys may be found representatives of virtually every major ecosystem on the planet. There are coral reefs and mangrove swamps on the coast, tropical rainforests on the western flanks, deserts in the north, dry scrublands to the east, and soaring above all in the clouds and blowing rain, the alpine tundra and the snowfields where the priests go to make prayers and offerings. Close to the equator, with twelve hours of daylight and twelve of darkness, with six months of rain and six months without, the Sierra Nevada de Santa Marta is a world in balance and harmony — exactly, the Indians maintain, as the Great Mother intended it to be.

According to myth, the mountains were dreamed into existence when the Great Mother spun her thoughts and conceived the nine layers of the universe. To stabilize the world, she thrust her spindle into its axis and lifted up the massif. Then, uncoiling a length of cotton thread, she delineated the horizons of the civilized world, tracing a circle around the base of the Sierra Nevada, which she declared to be the homeland of her children.

This primordial act of creation is never forgotten. The loom, the act of spinning, the notion of a community woven into the fabric of a landscape, are for the people of the Sierra vital and living metaphors that consciously guide and direct their lives. They survive as farmers, and in order to exploit diverse ecological zones, they are constantly on the move, harvesting manioc, maize, coffee, sugar, and pineapples in the hot lowlands, planting potatoes and onions in the cold mist of the cloud forests, climbing higher still to graze cattle and gather thatch. They refer to these periodic wanderings as threads, with the notion that over time a community lays down a protective cloak upon the earth. When they establish a garden, the women sow the southern half by planting in rows parallel to the sides of the plot. The men, responsible for the northern half, establish rows perpendicular to those laid down by the women, such that the two halves if folded one upon the other would produce a fabric. The garden is a piece of cloth. When the people pray they clasp in their hands small bundles of white cotton, symbols of the Great Mother who taught them to spin. The circular movement of hands in prayer recalls the moment when the Great Mother spun the universe into being. Her commandment was to protect everything she had woven. This was her law.

Those charged with the duty of leading all human beings in the ways of Serankua are the mamos, and their religious training is intense. The young acolytes are taken from their families at a young age, and then sequestered in a shadowy world of darkness, inside the *kan'kurua,* the men's temple, or in the immediate environs, for eighteen years — two periods of nine years that explicitly recall the nine months of gestation in a mother's womb. Throughout their initiation, the acolytes are in the womb of the Great Mother, and for all those years the world exists only as an abstraction. They are enculturated into the realm of the sacred as they learn that their rituals and prayers alone maintain the cosmic and ecological balance of the world. After his arduous transformation, the young man is taken on pilgrimage from the sea to the ice, from the cloud forests up through the rock and tussock grass to the *páramo,* the gateway to the heart of the world. For the first time in his life he sees the world not as an abstraction but as it actually exists in all its stunning beauty. The message is clear: It is his to protect.

From the coast he carries cotton, shells, and the pods of tropical plants to make *pagamientos,* or payments, at high sacred lakes where the wind is the breath of the Great Mother, and spirit guardians dwell, those with the responsibility of enforcing her laws. The offerings preserve life in all of its manifestations. The pure thoughts of the pilgrim are as seeds. From the páramo, he gathers to take back to the sea herbs and the leaves of *espeletia,* a plant known in Spanish as "the friar" because seen from a distance it can be mistaken for the silhouette of a man, a wandering monk lost in the swirling clouds and mist. Pilgrimage, movement through landscape, is for the Elder Brothers a constant gesture of affirmation that binds together humans and nature in a single web of reciprocity.

Since Columbus, the people of the Sierra have watched in horror as outsiders violate the Great Mother, tearing down the forests, which they perceive to be the skin and fabric of her body, to establish plantations of foreign crops — bananas and sugar cane, marijuana, and now coca for the illicit production of cocaine. Drawn by the profits of the coca trade, and pursued by the military, leftist guerrillas and right-wing paramilitaries have entered the Sierra and engulfed the Indians. To the Elders, this danger from below is echoed by a threat from on high. The snowfields and glaciers of the Sierra are receding at an alarming rate, transforming the mountain ecology. For us these may seem like quite unrelated developments. But for the Elders they are inextricably linked to each other and to the folly of the Younger Brothers, harbingers of the end of the world.

When I was last in the Sierra I travelled overland with the Arhuacos, a journey that began in their main centre of Nabusimake with a ritual purification, and then led to the sacred lakes and back to the sea. With me was Danilo Villafaña, son of Adalberto, an old friend of mine who was murdered by the paramilitaries. Danilo is today a political leader of the Arhuaco, but I remember him as an infant when I carried him on my back up and down the slopes of a then peaceful Sierra Nevada. Violence has been the backdrop of Danilo's life, and scores of Kogis, Wiwas, and Arhuacos have been killed by the FARC (the Fuerzas Armadas Revolucionarias de Colombia, the revolutionary armed forces of Colombia), slaughtered by the paramilitaries, or caught in crossfire by the army. Still the Indians cling to peace. As Danilo told me as we sat by a stream in Nabusimake, "The spiritual world, the world of mamos, and the world of guns do not go together."

When I returned from my pilgrimage I spoke with Ramon Gill, a highly respected Wiwa mamo. "The ancestors say," he told me, "that one day the Younger Brother will wake up. But only when the violence of nature is on top of him. That's when he'll wake up. What are we going to do? Well, we are not going to fight. We just want to make people understand. We are here speaking calmly so that hopefully the whole world will listen."

On January 9, 2004, at the height of the violence unleashed by the international consumption of cocaine, and after a two-year period that saw the death of several hundred Indian men and women in the Sierra, including many mamos, the Kogi, Wiwa, and Arhuaco issued a joint declaration: "Who will pay the universal mother for the air we breathe, the water that flows, the light of the sun? Everything that exists has a spirit that is sacred and must be respected. Our law is the law of origins, the law of life. We invite all the Younger Brothers to be guardians of life. We affirm our promise to the Mother, and issue a call for solidarity and unity for all peoples and all nations."

It is humbling to think that even as I write these words the mamos of the Elder Brothers, living just two hours by air from Miami Beach, are staring out to sea from the heights of the Sierra Nevada, praying for our well-being and that of the entire earth.

ONE'S INCLINATION UPON HEARING such an account is to dismiss it as being hopelessly naive or so impossibly beautiful as to be untrue. This, sadly, has too often been our response to cultures we encounter but do not understand, whose profound complexities are so dazzling as to overwhelm. When the British reached the shores of Australia, they were utterly unprepared for the sophistication of the place and its inhabitants, incapable of embracing its wonder. They had no understanding of the challenges of the desert, and little sensitivity to the achievement of Aboriginal people who, for over 55,000 years, had thrived as hunters and gatherers, and guardians of their world. In all that time the desire to improve upon the natural world, to tame the rhythm of the wild, had never touched them. The Aborigines accepted life as it was, a cosmological whole, the unchanging creation of the first dawn, when earth and sky separated and the original Ancestor, the Rainbow Serpent, brought into being all the primordial ancestors who through their thoughts, dreams, and journeys sang the world into existence.

The ancestors walked as they sang, and when it was time to stop, they slept. In their dreams they conceived the events of the following day, points of creation that fused one into another until every creature, every stream and stone, all space and time became part of the whole, the divine manifestation of the one great seminal impulse. When they grew exhausted from their labours, they retired into the earth, sky, clouds, rivers, lakes, plants, and animals of an island continent that still resonates with their memory. The paths taken by the Ancestors have never been forgotten. They are the Songlines, precise itineraries followed even today as the people travel across the template of the physical world.

As Aborigines track the Songlines and chant the stories of the first dawning, they become part of the Ancestors and enter Dreamtime, which is neither a dream nor a measure of the passage of time. It is the very realm of the ancestors, a parallel universe where the ordinary laws of time, space, and motion do not apply, where past, future, and present merge into one. It is a place Europeans can only approximate in sleep, and thus it became known to early English settlers as the Dreaming, or Dreamtime. But the term is misleading. A dream by Western definition is a state of consciousness divorced from the real world. Dreamtime, by contrast, is the real world, or at least one of two realities experienced in the daily lives of the Aborigines.

To walk the Songlines is to become part of the ongoing creation of the world, a place that both exists and is still being formed. Thus the Aborigines are not merely attached to the earth, they are essential to its existence. Without the land they would die. But without the people, the ongoing process of creation would cease and the earth would wither. Through movement and sacred rituals, the people maintain access to Dreamtime and play a dynamic and ongoing role in the world of the Ancestors.

A moment begins with nothing. A man or a woman walks, and from emptiness emerge the songs, the musical embodiment of reality, the cosmic melodies that give the world its character. The songs create vibrations that take shape. Dancing brings definition to the forms, and the objects of the phenomenological realm appear: trees, rocks, streams, all of them physical evidence of the Dreaming. Should the rituals stop, the voices fall silent, all would be lost. Everything on earth is held together by Songlines, everything is subordinate to the Dreaming, which is constant but ever changing. Every landmark is wedded to a memory of its origins, and yet always being born. Every animal and object resonates with the pulse of an ancient event, while still being dreamed into being. The world as it exists is perfect, though constantly in the process of being formed. The land is encoded with everything that has ever been, everything that ever will be, in every dimension of reality. To walk the land is to engage in a constant act of affirmation, an endless dance of creation.

The Europeans who washed ashore on the beaches of Australia in the last years of the eighteenth century lacked the language or imagination even to begin to understand the profound intellectual and spiritual achievements of the Aborigines. What they saw was a people who lived simply, whose technological achievements were modest, whose faces looked strange, whose habits were incomprehensible. The Aborigines lacked all the hallmarks of European civilization. They had no metal tools, knew nothing of writing, had never succumbed to the cult of the seed. Without agriculture or animal husbandry, they generated no surpluses, and thus had never embraced sedentary village life. Hierarchy and specialization were unknown. Their small semi-nomadic bands, living in temporary shelters made of sticks and grass, dependent on stone weapons, epitomized European notions of backwardness. For the British, in particular, it was inconceivable that a people could choose such a way of life. Progress and improvement through time were the hallmarks of the age, the essential ethos of Victorian life. To European eyes the Aborigines were the embodiment of savagery. An early French explorer described them as "the most miserable people of the world, human beings who approach closest to brute beast."

"They were nothing better than dogs," recalled Reverend William Yates in 1835, "and it was no more harm to shoot them than it would be to shoot a dog when he barked at you." Rationalizing the liberal use of the whip, an early settler in West Australia noted, "It should remembered that a native had a hide, and not an ordinary skin like ordinary human beings." Shot dead, the corpses of Aborigines were used as scarecrows, limp cadavers hung from the branches of trees. "Their doom," wrote Anthony Trollope in 1870, "is to be exterminated, the sooner the better." As recently as 1902 an elected politician, King O'Malley, rose in Parliament to declare: "There is no scientific evidence that the aboriginal is a human being at all."

By stipulation of the Native Administration Act of 1936, no native in West Australia could move without permission of the state. No Aboriginal father or mother was permitted legal custody of a child. Aboriginal people could be ordered into reserves and institutions or banished from towns. The government had final say over the legitimacy and legality of any marriage. As recently as the 1960s, one school textbook, *A Treasury of Australian Fauna*, included the Aborigines among the more interesting animals of the country.

By the early years of the twentieth century a combination of disease, exploitation, and murder had reduced the Aboriginal population from well over a million at the time of European contact to a mere thirty thousand. In little over a century, a land bound together by Songlines, where the people moved effortlessly from one dimension to the next, from the future to the past, and from the past to the present, was transformed from Eden to Armageddon.

Knowing what we do today of the extraordinary reach of the Aboriginal mind, the subtlety of their thoughts and philosophy, and the evocative power of their rituals, it is chilling to think of this reservoir of human potential, wisdom, intuition, and insight that very nearly ran dry during those terrible days of death and conflagration. As it is, Aborigine languages, which may have numbered 270 at the time of contact, and may have had more than 600 dialects, are disappearing at the rate of one or more a year. Half have been lost, and only 18 are today spoken by as many as 500 individuals.

In truth, the visionary realm of the Aboriginal peoples of Australia represented one of the great experiments in human thought. Descendants of the first wave of humans to leave Africa, the first peoples of Australia arrived on an island continent that had been geographically isolated from the rest of world for over a hundred million years. They encountered an austere and impossible place, the driest land mass on earth, where evolution itself had taken a bizarre turn, producing plants and animals unlike any other: egg-laying mammals, giant flightless birds, and a host of creatures that nursed their embryos outside the womb in the safety of a marsupial pouch. Among the first animals the Aboriginal peoples saw, perhaps even at sea during one of the open crossings, were saltwater crocodiles 8 metres long, primordial creatures that could see, hear, and breathe when almost totally submerged. These reptiles hunted by stealth, killing anything they could overpower, and would have welcomed, though not warmly, a new form of prey.

Once on land, the people went walking. Through time, small extended family bands reached to every corner of the continent, establishing clan territories, which became loosely associated through common language into larger networks or tribes. The size of the clan territories depended on the carrying capacity of the land. The grasslands and eucalyptus groves of the south and east had relatively large concentrations of people. The central and western deserts were so sparsely settled that men were as shadows on the sand. By the time of European contact there were as many as 10,000 distinct spheres of spiritual and societal focus, 10,000 homelands, each aggressively defended by boys raised to be warriors.

The boundaries of the clans, both geographic and cultural, were defined by sacred places, by narratives linking people and ancestors, and by a web of social relations so intricate it would take Western anthropologists a century even to begin to chart its complexity. There were over a hundred named kin relationships, each implying specific rights and obligations, rules and regulations of blood and marriage that established a social map allowing every individual to know at all times how he or she was expected to behave. In place of technological wizardry, our great achievement, the Aboriginal people of Australia invented a matrix of connectivity. In doing so, they generated a protective shell as daunting, comforting, and complete as the city walls we erect with similar motivation to insulate our lives from the vicissitudes of nature.

Within the clan territories, individuals developed a localized knowledge of place that was extraordinary. I recently spent a month in the remote reaches of Arnhem Land in the Northern Territory of Australia with a remarkable man, Otto Bulmaniya Campion, and his extended family – his wife Christine, his uncle Geoffrey, all the kids – out on the land. I wanted to know about the Dreaming and the Songlines, something more than I had learned from books. At first I asked questions, sought definitions, but then, recognizing my folly, I simply watched.

Arriving at a billabong, a pond or slough, a place to camp, Otto and the lads immediately set fire to the grass, both to cleanse and to regenerate the site. As they bathed they beat the water, sending a message to the crocodiles. They then purified themselves with the smoke from ironwood branches, and with their hands wrapped a ring of mud and red ochre around the trunk of every tree. In a few gestures they domesticated the space, sweeping the ground with branches, erecting windbreaks, peeling off great sheets of paper bark from the *melaleuca* trees to serve as bedding and blankets. The mothers and young children slept in one circle, the elder men in another, and young single boys in yet a third. When they went after *barramundi* fish, they kept up a constant dialogue, describing the nature of their hunger and needs, invoking the ancestors and the spirit of the ancestors of the fish. Food they called *bush tucker,* and it could be anything – green ants, flying fox, geese, or wild yams. When they hunted, they covered their bodies in mud, masking their scent, becoming as one with the prey. One morning, Christine and Otto's son painted themselves in red ochre, a ritual compact that allowed the boy to become transformed into the image of the Rainbow Serpent.

Around the fire at night, Otto conversed with his father's spirit, a voice that came out of the flames. By day he tracked kangaroo with an intense deductive logic that would have put Sherlock Holmes to shame. But once the animal was dead, he reverted to reverence, a strict protocol that dictated precisely how the carcass had to be treated lest the direst of calamities befall the hunter and his community. The tongue is carefully extracted so that children grow to speak properly and with respect. The legs are broken at the knee to liberate the animal's spirit, and then folded and bound in a specific order and manner. The gut is cut open to reveal parasitic worms, eaten raw, flavoured only by the green roughage extracted from the stomach. The distribution of the meat reflects the authority of kinship, head to the hunter, tail to the brother-in-law, hindquarters to second and third brothers.

As we walked the land together I was astonished not only by the depth of Otto's knowledge, but even more so by his way of knowing. His thinking was completely non-linear, a sort of magical pattern of what seemed to be free association. A trail of ants would lead to sweat bees, a comb of honey dug from the ground prompted a reference to a mythic bird, talk of a spirit, which in turn brought us back to the Morningstar Songline, Rock Wallaby Dreaming, and the utility of the paperbark tree, a source of shelter and so much more. Kapok trees coming into bloom implied that baby kangaroos, or joeys, have enough hair to survive the death of their mothers. A yellow-red blossom on an unknown tree, with a colour suggestive of the fat of an emu, revealed to Otto the proper time to hunt the long-necked turtle.

I came to realize, simply by being with Otto and his family, that in a sense the Aboriginal peoples had never been truly nomadic. To the contrary, they lived locked within the territories delineated by their ancestors. This was a revelation. Imagine for a moment if all the genius and intellect of all the generations that have come before you had been concentrated on a single set of tasks, focused exclusively on knowing a particular piece of ground, not only the plants and animals but every ecological, climatic, geographic detail, the pulse of every sentient creature, the rhythm of every breath of wind, the patterns of every season. This was the norm in Aboriginal Australia.

What linked the clan territories was not the physical movement of peoples but rather the strength of a common idea, a subtle but universal philosophy, a way of thinking. This was the Dreaming. It refers on one level, as we have seen, to the first dawning, when the Rainbow Serpent and all the ancestral beings created the world. And it is remembered in the Songlines, which are the trajectories that these ancestors travelled as they sang the world into being.

But the Songlines, I discovered from Otto, are not straight or linear. They do not even necessarily exist in three-dimensional space. In their numbers, however, they weave a web across an entire continent. For a civilization that lacked the written word they became a record of the past, a promise of the future, and a network that in the moment bound together all of the people. The goal of the individual, as Otto taught me, is not to follow the Songline from beginning to end, but to honour the ancestors at the points of power and memory that mark the passage of a Songline through one's particular clan territory.

But, critically, the Dreaming is not a myth or a memory. It is what happened at the time of creation, but also what happens now, and what will happen for all eternity. In the Aboriginal universe there is no past, present, or future. In not one of the hundreds of dialects spoken at the moment of contact was there a word for time. There is no notion of linear progression, no goal of improvement, no idealization of the possibility of change. To the contrary, the entire logos of the Dreaming is stasis, constancy, balance, and consistency. The entire purpose of humanity is not to improve anything. It is to engage in the ritual and ceremonial activities deemed to be essential for the maintenance of the world precisely as it was at the moment of creation. Imagine if all of Western intellectual and scientific passion had focused from the beginning of time on keeping the Garden of Eden precisely as it was when Adam and Eve had their fateful conversation.

The universe of the Aboriginal people was no ideal world. Conflicts were violent. The rituals could be austere in the extreme. The acquisition of initiatory knowledge among the Warlpiri, to cite but one example, involved the cutting and transformation of the male sexual organ, a vertical incision that ultimately left the penis fully splayed. But the overriding mood of the civilization, as W.E.H. Stanner described, was one of acceptance of belief. There was little place for skepticism, inquiry, or dissent. The Dreaming, as he wrote, "defined what was, determined what is, embodied all that can be."

In the Western tradition existence is something to be contemplated. Our thinkers and philosophers step outside of life to discern abstract ideas that we define as insights. The Dreaming makes such reflection both meaningless and impossible. It envelops the individual in a web of belief and conviction from which there is no exit, for one cannot think that one's thoughts are wrong. To violate a law of the Dreaming is a transgression not limited to the moment, but rather one that reverberates through all dimensions, through the eternal past and the limitless future. The Aborigines, as Stanner understood, were not a people without a history. They were, he wrote, a civilization that in a sense had defeated history.

The Dreaming answered both the questions how and why. It dictated the way a person must live. Man's obligation was not to improve upon nature, but to sustain the world. The literal preservation of the land was the most fundamental priority of every Aboriginal man and woman. It was a profoundly conservative ideology. I am not saying whether it was right or wrong, good or bad. But it had consequences. Clearly, had humanity as a whole followed the ways of the Aborigines, the intellectual track laid down by these descendants of the first humans to walk out of Africa, we would not have put a man on the moon. But, on the other hand, had the Dreaming become a universal devotion, we would not be contemplating today the consequences of industrial processes that by any scientific definition threaten the very life supports of the planet.

THIS STORY, LIKE ALL NARRATIVES, weaves its way back to the beginning. I opened this lecture by speaking of the

Sacred Headwaters, this astonishingly beautiful and rare jewel of a valley from which are born the salmon rivers of home — actually of *my* home, for the Stikine is where I live. The people of the Stikine River valley, one of the most extraordinary places I have ever known, have rallied against these projects, for they have a very different way of thinking about the land. For them the Sacred Headwaters is a neighbourhood, at once their grocery store and sanctuary, their church and schoolyard, their cemetery and country club. They believe that the people with greatest claim to ownership of the valley are the generations as yet unborn. The Sacred Headwaters will be their nursery. The Iskut elders, almost all of whom grew up on the land, have formally called for an end to all industrial activity in the valley and the creation of a Sacred Headwaters Tribal Heritage Area.

Since the summer of 2005, Iskut men, women and children, together with Tahltan and First Nations supporters from Telegraph Creek and beyond, have maintained in all seasons an educational camp at the head of the only road access to the Sacred Headwaters. Those who would violate the land they hold in trust have been denied entry. Those who accept and revere the land as it is have been welcomed. With everyone they have shared their vision of a new era of sustainable stewardship for their homeland and for the entire northwest quadrant of the province. After so many years on the line, they are not about to give up. In the end, what is at stake is the future of one of the most extraordinary regions in all of North America. The fate of the Sacred Headwaters transcends the interests of local residents, provincial agencies, mining companies, and those few who favour industrial development at any cost. No amount of methane gas, coal or copper can compensate for the sacrifice of a place that can be the Sacred Headwaters of all Canadians, and indeed of all peoples of the world. This, ultimately, is the message of the Elder Brothers.

FIVE

CENTURY OF THE WIND

"The ideal of a single civilization for everyone implicit in the cult of progress and technique impoverishes and mutilates us. Every view of the world that becomes extinct, every culture that disappears, diminishes a possibility of life." — Octavio Paz

THE GARDEN OF EDEN has been found, and it lies on the southwest coast of Africa, not far from the homeland of the Juwasi Bushmen who for generations lived in open truce with the lions of the Kalahari. Humanity's point of departure from Africa has also been located with some precision, on the other side of the ancient continent, on the western shore of the Red Sea. From there we walked through desert sands and over snow-covered passes, through jungles and mountain streams, eventually finding our way across oceans and wind-stripped coral atolls to black sand beaches that fronted entire continents of untold mysteries and latent hopes. We settled the Arctic and the Himalaya, the grasslands of the Asian steppe and the boreal forests of the north, where winter winds blow so fierce that willow sap freezes and caribou graze on branches dead to the sun. On the rivers of India we encountered sounds that echoed the human heart, and in the searing silences of the Sahara we found water. Along the way we invented ten thousand different ways of being.

In the mountains of Oaxaca in Mexico the Mazatec learned to communicate across vast distances by whistling, mimicking the intonations of their tonal language to create a vocabulary written on the wind. Along the beaches of Dahomey, Vodoun acolytes opened wide the windows of the mystic, discovering the power of trance, allowing human beings to move in and out of the spirit realm with ease and impunity. In the forests of Yunnan, Naxi shaman carved mystical tales into rocks, while in the Orinoco River delta their counterparts among the Warao endured nicotine narcosis in their quest for visions and inspiration, knowledge of the Lords of the Rain, the House of the Swallow-Tailed Kite, the heraldic raptor, and the dancing jaguar.

Off the shore of Sumatra on the island of Siberut, the Mentawai people recognized that spirits enliven everything that exists — birds, plants, clouds, even the rainbows that arch across the sky. Rejoicing in the beauty of the world, these divine entities could not possibly be expected to reside in a human body that was not itself beautiful. Thus the Mentawai came to believe that if nature lost its lustre, if the landscape became drab, if they themselves as a physical presence in creation ceased to do honour to the essence of beauty, the primordial forces of creation would abandon this realm for the settlements of the dead, and all life would perish. To respect the ancestors and celebrate the living, the Mentawai, both men and women, devote their lives to the pursuit of aesthetic beauty, preening their bodies, filing their teeth, adding brilliant feathers to their hair, and inscribing delicate spiral patterns on their bodies. In daily life they approach every task, however mundane, fully adorned.

In the mountains of Japan, outside of Kyoto, Tendai monks sleep for two hours a day and, with only a bowl of noodles and a rice ball for food, run through the sacred cryptomeria forests seventeen hours at a stretch for seven years, covering at one point in their Kaihigyo initiation 80 kilometres a day for one hundred days. As a final ordeal they must go without food, water, and sleep for nine days, even as they sit in silent meditation, their bodies exposed to the roaring heat of a bonfire. Tradition dictates that those who fail to complete the training must end their lives. Beneath their white robes they carry a knife and a rope. Slung from their back are rope sandals. They wear out five pairs in a day. In the last four centuries only forty-six men have completed the ordeal, a ritual path of enlightenment that brings the initiate closer to the realm of the dead, all with the goal of revealing to the living that everyone and everything are equal, that human beings are not exceptional, that nothing in this world is permanent.

PEOPLE OFTEN ASK WHY it matters if these wondrous yet exotic cultures and their belief systems disappear. What importance does it have to a family in Vancouver or Halifax, on a Saskatchewan farm or living in the embrace and comfort of a Newfoundland cove, if some distant tribe in Africa is extinguished through assimilation or violence, if their dreams and spiritual passions articulated through ritual turn to vapour? The query, as you might guess if you've had a chance to reflect on the first four of these Massey Lectures, confounds me. If someone needs to ask that question, can he or she possibly be expected to understand the answer?

Does it matter to the people of Quebec if the Tuareg of the Sahara lose their culture? Probably not. No more than the loss of Quebec would matter to the Tuareg. But I would argue that the loss of either way of life does matter to humanity as a whole. On the one hand it is a basic issue of human rights. Who is to say that the Canadian perspective on reality matters more than that of the Tuareg? And at a more fundamental level we have to ask ourselves: What kind of world do we want to live in? Most Canadians will never encounter a camel caravan of blue-robed Tuareg moving slowly across an ocean of white sand. For that matter most of us will never see a painting by Monet, or hear a Mozart symphony. But does this mean that the world would not be a lesser place without these artists and cultures and their unique interpretations of reality?

So I respond with a metaphor from biology. What does it matter if a single species of life becomes extinct? Well, imagine you are getting onto an airplane, and you notice that the mechanic is popping out the rivets in the wings. You ask the obvious question and the mechanic says, "No problem. We save money with each rivet and so far we've had no problems." Perhaps the loss of a single rivet makes no difference, but eventually the wings fall off. It is the same thing with culture. If the marathon monks cease to run, or if the children of the Mentawai shift their sense of beauty to something more mundane and uninspired, or if the Naxi shaman no longer write in stone and abandon their native script, Dongba, the world's last living hieroglyphic language, will the sky fall? No. But we're not talking about the loss of a single species of life or a single cultural adaptation. We are speaking about a waterfall of destruction unprecedented in the history of our species. In our lifetime half of the voices of humanity are being silenced.

The problem is not change. We have this conceit in the West that while we have been celebrating and developing technological wizardry, somehow the other peoples of the world have been static and intellectually idle. Nothing could be further from the truth. Change is the one constant in history. All peoples in all places are always dancing with new possibilities for life. Nor is technology per se a threat to the integrity of culture. The Lakota did not stop being Sioux when they gave up the bow and arrow for the rifle any more than a rancher from Medicine Hat ceased being a Canadian when he gave up the horse and buggy in favour of the automobile. It is neither change nor technology that threatens the integrity of culture. It is power, the crude face of domination. We have this idea that these indigenous peoples, these distant others, quaint and colourful though they may be, are somehow destined to fade away, as if by natural law, as if they are failed attempts at being modern, failed attempts at being us. This is simply not true. In every case these are dynamic living peoples being driven out of existence by identifiable and overwhelming external forces. This is actually an optimistic observation, for it suggests that if human beings are the agents of cultural destruction, we can also be the facilitators of cultural survival.

To gain perspective on this clash of power and culture, let's turn for a moment to the history of our own continent and the experience of a single First Nation, the Kiowa. Originally a hunting and gathering people from the headwaters of the Missouri River, the Kiowa came down from the mountains to the grasslands of the Dakotas about a century before the American Revolution. They encountered the Crow, who taught them the religion and culture of the Plains, the divinity of the Sun, the ways of the buffalo, the power and utility of the horse. They later moved north into the Black Hills, where they fought the Lakota, before fleeing south, driven by the

Cheyenne and Arapaho across the headwaters of the Arkansas. There the Kiowa clashed with the Comanche, before forging an alliance that gave the two nations control of the southern grasslands and the vast herds of buffalo that moved as shadows across the continent.

Once each year, at the height of summer when down appeared on the cottonwood trees, the people came together for the Sun Dance, a time of spiritual renewal. The teepees went up in a wide circle, the entire encampment oriented to the rising sun. The medicine lodge was the focal point, for within it, on a stick planted on the western side, hung the *Tai-me,* the sacred image of the sun. It was a simple fetish, a small human figure with a face of green stone, a robe of white feathers, and a headdress of ermine skin and a single erect feather. Around its neck were strands of blue beads, and painted on its face, neck, and back were the symbols of the sun and the moon. For the Kiowa the Tai-me was the source of life itself. Kept in a rawhide box under the protection of a hereditary Keeper, it was never exposed to the light save for the four days of the Sun Dance. At that time its power spread into all and everything present: the children and the warrior dancers, the buffalo skull that lay at its base as the animals' representative of the sun, the Ten Medicines Bundles displayed before it, the men who for four days and nights slowly turned their shields to follow the passing sun, the young dancer who stared at the sun all day every day sacrificing his vision that the people might come to see.

As late as 1871, buffalo outnumbered people in North America. In that year one could stand on a bluff in the Dakotas and see buffalo in every direction for 50 kilometres. Herds were so large it took days for them to pass by. Wyatt Earp described one herd of over a million animals stretched over a grazing area the size of the state of Rhode Island. Within nine years of that sighting, the buffalo had vanished from the Plains. U.S. government policy was explicit. Exterminate the buffalo and destroy the cultures of the Plains. Theodore Roosevelt, revered today by conservationists, expressed the national mood. "The settler and pioneer have justice on their side; this great continent could not have been kept as nothing but a game preserve for squalid savages."

In less than a decade the systematic slaughter reduced the bison to a zoological curiosity, and destroyed all native resistance. General Philip Sheridan, who orchestrated the campaign, advised the U.S. Congress to mint a commemorative medal, with a dead buffalo on one side, and a dead Indian on the other. On July 20, 1890, the Sun Dance was officially outlawed, and on pain of imprisonment the Kiowa and all the Plains cultures were denied their essential act of faith. An outbreak of measles and influenza in the spring of 1892 struck a final blow.

What transpired on the American frontier was repeated throughout the world. In 1879 in Argentina, General Roca launched the Conquest of the Desert, a military campaign, which had as its expressed goal the extermination of the Indians of the Pampa and the seizure of their lands and cattle. The people of Tasmania were annihilated within seventy-five years of contact. The Reverend John West, a Christian missionary, rationalized the slaughter as the necessary cleansing of the land of an offensive people he described as a "detested incubus." The colonial administration of French Polynesia in 1850 as a matter of principle formally banned all expressions of Polynesian culture, inter-island trade and voyaging, ritual prayer and feasting, tattooing, wood carving, dancing, and even singing. In 1884 British colonial authorities outlawed the potlatch in the Pacific Northwest. A year later, as European delegates gathered at the Congress of Berlin to carve up the African continent, they formally pledged their support for all efforts "calculated to educate the natives and to teach them to understand and appreciate the benefits of civilization." The follow-up conference leading to the Brussels Act of 1892 called on colonial powers throughout the world to "bring about the extinction of barbarous customs."

That same year the first of 40,000 Bora and Huitoto Indians died in the Northwest Amazon, along the Río Putumayo, murdered by the traders and overseers of the Anglo-Peruvian Rubber Company. In the Congo Free State, King Leopold's private armies, again in pursuit of latex, the white blood of the forest, slaughtered as many as 8 million Africans. In 1919, in the immediate wake of the First World War, a global conflict that had obliterated European youth and violated every notion of decency and honour, the victors gathered in Paris, and by the terms of article 22 of the League of Nations Covenant, placed tribal peoples, all those incapable of withstanding the "strenuous conditions of the modern world," under their tutelage as a "sacred trust of civilization." In the hundred years leading up to the war, indigenous peoples had been forced to surrender to colonial powers lands spanning nearly half the globe. Millions had died, victims of the very civilization that in its own spasms of self-destruction would twice, in little more than a generation, come close to immolating the entire world.

This legacy of dispossession, in what Eduardo Galeano called "the century of the wind," reminds us that these fateful events happened not in the distant past but in the lifetimes of our own grandparents, and they continue to this day. Genocide, the physical extermination of a people, is universally condemned. Ethnocide, the destruction of a people's way of life, is in many quarters sanctioned and endorsed as appropriate development policy. Modernity provides the rationale for disenfranchisement, with the real goal too often being the extraction of natural resources on an industrial scale from territories occupied for generations by indigenous peoples whose ongoing presence on the land proves to be an inconvenience.

THE MOUTH OF THE BARAM RIVER in Borneo is the colour of the earth. To the north, the soils of Sarawak disappear into the South China Sea and fleets of empty Japanese freighters hang on the horizon, awaiting the tides and a chance to fill their holds with raw logs ripped from the forests of Borneo. The river settlements are settings of opportunity and despair — muddy logging camps and clusters of shanties, their leprous facades patched with sheets of metal, plastic, and scavenged boards. Children by the river's edge dump barrels of garbage, which drifts back to shore in the wake of each passing log barge. For kilometres the river is choked with debris and silt, and along its banks lie thousands of logs stacked thirty deep, some awaiting shipment, some slowly rotting in the tropical heat.

Some 150 kilometres upriver is another world, a varied and magical landscape of forest and soaring mountains, dissected by crystalline rivers and impregnated by the world's most extensive network of caves and underground passages. This is the traditional territory of the Penan, a culture of hunters and gatherers often said to be among the last nomadic peoples of Southeast Asia. In myth and in daily life they celebrate the bounty of a forest whose biological richness and diversity surpasses that of even the most prolific regions of the Amazon. In a series of plots comprising a total area of but a single square kilometre of Borneo woodland, less than a fortieth the area of Vancouver's Stanley Park, have been found as many species of trees as exist in all of North America.

The term *nomadic* is somewhat misleading, implying a life of constant movement and with it perhaps a dearth of fidelity to place. In fact, the Penan passage through the forest is cyclical and resource dependent, with the same sites being occupied time and again over the lifetime of an individual. Thus the forest is for them a series of neighbourhoods, wild and potentially dangerous in certain ways, but fundamentally domesticated by generations of human presence and interaction. Every feature of the landscape resonates with a story. Every point along a trail, every boulder and cave, each one of the more than two thousand streams that run through their lands has a name. A sense of stewardship permeates Penan society, dictating consistently the manner in which the people utilize and apportion the environment. Individual resources, a clump of sago, fruit trees, dart-poison trees, fishing sites, medicinal plants are affiliated with individual kin groups, and these familial rights acknowledged by all pass down through the generations. "From the forest," they say very simply, "we get our life."

What most impressed me when I first visited the Penan in 1989 was a certain quality of being, an essential humanity that was less innate than a consequence of the manner in which they had chosen to live their lives. They had little sense of time, save for the rhythms of the natural world, the fruiting seasons of plants, the passage of the sun and moon, the sweat bees that emerge two hours before dusk, the black cicadas that electrify the forest at precisely six every evening. They had no notion of paid employment, of work as burden, as opposed to leisure as recreation. For them, there was only life, the daily round. Children learned not in school but through experience, often at the side of their parents. With families and individuals often widely dispersed, self-sufficiency was the norm, with everyone capable of doing every necessary task. So there was very little sense of hierarchy.

How do you measure wealth in a society in which there are no specialists, in which everyone can make everything from raw materials readily found in the forest, a society in which there is no incentive to accumulate material possessions because everything has to be carried on the back? The Penan explicitly perceive wealth as the strength of social relations among people, for should these relationships weaken or fray, all will suffer. Should conflict lead to a schism and families go their separate ways for prolonged periods, both groups may starve for want of sufficient hunters. Thus, as in many hunting and gathering societies, direct criticism of another is frowned upon. The priority is always the solidarity of the group. Confrontation and displays of anger are exceedingly rare. Civility and humour are the norm.

There is no word for "thank you" in their language because sharing is an obligation. One never knows who will be the next to bring food to the fire. I once gave a cigarette to an elderly woman and watched as she tore it apart to distribute equitably the individual strands of tobacco to each shelter in the encampment, rendering the product useless but honouring her duty to share. When, some time after my first visit, a number of Penan came to Canada to campaign for the protection of their forests, nothing impressed them more than homelessness. They could not understand how in a place as wealthy as

Vancouver such a thing could exist. A Canadian or American grows up believing that homelessness is a regrettable but inevitable feature of life. The Penan live by the adage that a poor man shames us all. Indeed, the greatest transgression in their culture is *sihun,* a concept that essentially means a failure to share.

The Penan lacked the written word; the total vocabulary of the language at any point in time was always the knowledge of the best storyteller. This too had consequences. Writing, while clearly an extraordinary innovation in human history, is by definition brilliant shorthand that permits and even encourages the numbing of memory. Oral traditions sharpen recollection, even as they seem to open a certain mysterious dialogue with the natural world. Just as we can hear the voices of characters when we read a novel, the Penan perceive the voices of animals in the forest. Every forest sound is an element of a language of the spirit. Trees bloom when they hear the lovely song of the bare-throated krankaputt. Birds heard from a certain direction bear good tidings; the same sounds heard from a different direction may be a harbinger of ill. Entire hunting parties may be turned back to camp by the call of a banded kingfisher, the cry of a bat hawk. Other birds, like the spiderhunter, guide the Penan to a kill. Before embarking on a long journey they must see a white-headed hawk and hear the call of the crested rainbird and the doglike sound of the barking deer.

This remarkable dialogue informs Penan life in ways that few outsiders can be expected to understand. But one who did was Bruno Manser, a Swiss activist who lived among the Penan for six years, and later returned to their homeland where he died in mysterious circumstances. "Every morning at dawn," Bruno wrote, "gibbons howl and their voices carry for great distances, riding the thermal boundary created by the cool of the forest and the warm air above as the sun strikes the canopy. Penan never eat the eyes of gibbons. They are afraid of losing themselves in the horizon. They lack an inner horizon. They don't separate dreams from reality. If someone dreams that a tree limb falls on the camp, they will move with the dawn."

Tragically, by the time Bruno disappeared in 2000, his fate uncertain, the sounds of the forest had become the sounds of machinery. Throughout the 1980s, as the plight of the Amazon rainforest captured the attention of the world, Brazil produced less than 3 percent of tropical timber exports. Malaysia accounted for nearly 60 percent of production, much of it from Sarawak and the homeland of the Penan. The commercial harvesting of timber along the northern coast of Borneo only began, and on a small scale, after the Second World War. By 1971 Sarawak was exporting 4.2 million cubic metres of wood annually, much of it from the upland forests of the hinterland. In 1990 the annual cut had escalated to 18.8 million cubic metres. In 1993, when I returned for a second visit to the Penan, there were thirty logging companies operating in the Baram River drainage alone, some equipped with as many as twelve hundred bulldozers, working on over a million acres of forested land traditionally belonging to the Penan and their immediate neighbours. Fully 70 percent of Penan lands were formally designated by the government to be logged. Illegal operations threatened much of the rest.

Within a single generation the Penan world was turned upside down. Women raised in the forest found themselves working as servants or prostitutes in logging camps that muddied the rivers with debris and silt, making fishing impossible. Children in government settlement camps who had never suffered the diseases of civilization succumbed to measles and influenza. The Penan elected to resist, blockading the logging roads with rattan barricades. It was a brave yet quixotic gesture, blowpipes against bulldozers, and ultimately no match for the power of the Malaysian state.

The government's position was unequivocal. "It is our policy," noted Prime Minister Mahathir bin Mohamad, "to eventually bring all jungle dwellers into the mainstream. There is nothing romantic about these helpless, half-starved disease-ridden people." James Wong, then Sarawak's minister for housing and public health, added: "We don't want them running around like animals. No one has the ethical right to deprive the Penan of the right to assimilation into Malaysian society."

This was the essence of the government's position. Nomadic people were an embarrassment to the nation-state. In order to emancipate the Penan from their backwardness, the government had to free them from who they actually were. Indigenous peoples like the Penan are said to stand in the way of development, which becomes grounds for dispossessing them and destroying their way of life. Their disappearance is then described as inevitable, as such archaic folk cannot be expected to survive in the twenty-first century.

"Is it right to deny them the advancement of the modern world?" asked an exasperated Lim Keng Yaik, Malaysian minister for primary commodities. "Let them choose to live the way they want to. Let them stay at the Waldorf Astoria in New York for two years with the amenities of Cadillacs, air conditioners, and beautiful juicy steaks at their table every day. Then when they come back, let them make the choice whether they want to live in the style of New Yorkers or as natural Penan in the tropical rain forests."

In 1992 a Penan delegation did in fact travel to New York, though it did not, as I recall, stay at the Waldorf. On December 10, Anderson Mutang Urud addressed the UN General Assembly. "The government," he began, "says that it is bringing us development. But the only development that we see is dusty logging roads and relocation camps. For us, their so-called progress means only starvation, dependence, helplessness, the destruction of our culture, and the demoralization of our people. The government says it is creating jobs for our people. Why do we need jobs? My father and grandfather did not have to ask the government for jobs. They were never unemployed. They lived from the land and from the forest. It was a good life. We were never hungry or in need. These logging jobs will disappear with the forest. In ten years all the jobs will be gone and the forest that has sustained us for thousands of years will be gone with them."

As recently as 1960, seven years after I was born, the vast majority of the Penan lived as nomads. When I returned in 1998 for a third visit perhaps a hundred families still lived exclusively in the forest. Only a year ago I received a note from Ian Mackenzie, a Canadian linguist who has dedicated his academic life to the study of the Penan language. Ian confirmed that the very last of the families had settled. The basis of the existence of one of the most extraordinary nomadic cultures in the world had been destroyed. Throughout the traditional homeland of the Penan, the sago and rattan, the palms, lianas, and fruit trees lie crushed on the forest floor. The hornbill has fled with the pheasants, and as the trees continue to fall, a unique way of life, morally inspired, inherently right, and effortlessly pursued for centuries, has collapsed in a single generation.

THE FIRST TIME I VISITED the Khmer temple of Angkor Wat in Cambodia I met an elderly Buddhist nun whose feet and hands had been severed from her body during the era of Pol Pot and the killing fields. Her crime had been her faith, and her punishment the barbaric response of a regime and an ideology that denied all nuances of spiritual belief and indeed the very notion of ethnicity and culture. Reducing the infinite permutations of human society and consciousness to a simple opposition of owners and workers, capitalist and proletariat, Marxism, formulated by a German philosopher in the Reading Room of the British Library, was in a sense the perfect triumph of the mechanistic view of existence inspired by Descartes. Society itself was a machine that could be engineered for the betterment of all. This was precisely what Pol Pot, Brother Number One, had in mind. He thought he was helping, moving history forward, even if it meant the death of 3 million. The attempt of revolutionary cadre in scores of nations to impose Marxist thought, this European idea, on peoples as diverse as the Nenets reindeer herders of Siberia, the Dogon living beneath the burial caves of their ancestors in the cliffs of Mali, the Mongolian descendants of Genghis Khan, the Laotians and Vietnamese, the Bantu, Bambara, and Fulani would appear almost laughably naive had not the consequences proved so disastrous for so much of humanity. "Anyone who thinks they alone can change the world," Peter Matthiessen once wrote, "is both wrong and dangerous." Surely he had in mind men such as Pol Pot, Stalin, Hitler, and Mao Zedong.

In what Winston Churchill called the "bloodstained century of violence," Mao Zedong bears the dark distinction of being the political leader most successful in killing his own people. When Mao famously whispered into the ear of a young Dalai Lama that all religion was poison, the Tibetan spiritual leader knew what was coming. The Great Leap Forward, an egregiously ill-conceived campaign to collectivize all production and make China the largest steel producer in the world, caused the death by famine of 40 million Chinese in 1959. That same year the People's Liberation Army marched into Lhasa, fully intent on the destruction of the Tibetan Buddhist tradition.

Ideological fanaticism, materialist thought control, and communist class struggle reached a watershed during the Cultural Revolution, unleashed by Mao in 1966. Its goal was the creation of a pure socialist cadre, men and women whose minds had been purged and memories erased to yield a template upon which the thoughts of Mao could be engraved. The true and just society would emerge in the wake of the destruction of the Four Olds: old ideas, old culture, old customs, and old habits. Create the new by smashing the old. This was the official slogan of what was heralded to be the last battle before the coming of the socialist paradise.

All notions of religion and spirit, the poetics of culture and family, intuitions about the relationship of man and woman and nature, the scent of the soil, and the meaning of rain falling upon stones had no place in Mao's calculus of transformation and domination. Nationality was considered a mere product of economic disparity. Once material inequalities had been addressed, ethnic distinctions would wither. Tibet, of course, exemplified the old; China, the new. Thus, the Cultural Revolution both implied and demanded a total assault on every facet of Tibet's ancient civilization. Over a million Tibetans were killed, and in time 6,000 monasteries and temples, *chörtens* and religious shrines were reduced to rubble, blasted from the air and ground by artillery and bombs. Imagine for a moment how we might feel as Canadians if something like this happened to our country, if a nation inordinately more powerful were to invade, declare our religious beliefs to be anathema, and proceed to destroy all of our churches, synagogues, temples, and mosques. I stress that the problem was not of the Chinese people, who more than any suffered under Mao. The insanity came about because of an idea, which grew from another layer of violence, a pressure created by colonial history and the unexpected and uncontrollable outcomes of a chaotic cultural encounter.

This history was very much on my mind when I travelled a number of years ago in the Himalaya with two friends, Matthieu Ricard and Sherab Barma. Matthieu, an inspired writer and photographer, did advanced post-graduate studies in molecular biology at the Institut Pasteur in Paris before leaving the academic world some forty years ago to take vows as a Tibetan monk. For more than a decade he was the student and personal aide of Khyentse Rinpoche, a revered spiritual lama of the Nyingma tradition, and today from his base at the Shechen Monastery in Katmandu, Matthieu remains a confidant and translator of His Holiness the Dalai Lama. Sherab is a traditional Tibetan doctor, whose seven-year training included a twelve-month solitary retreat in a cave to which he returns each year for a month of meditation. The three of us met at Chiwong, a beautiful monastery that clings like a swallow's nest to the flank of the Himalaya in Nepal. From there we went to the sanctuary of Thubten Choling, home to some 800 monks and nuns who devote their lives to personal transformation and what Matthieu calls "the science of the mind that is Tibetan Buddhism." The use of this phrase intrigued me, especially as Matthieu had at one point in his life pursued a career in scientific research and had worked in the lab of François Jacob, a Nobel laureate.

"What is science," he said one morning, "but the empirical pursuit of the truth? What is Buddhism but 2,500 years of direct observation as to the nature of mind? A lama once told me that Western science and efficiency has made a major contribution to minor needs. We spend all of our lifetimes trying to live to be a hundred without losing our hair or teeth. The Buddhist spends his lifetime trying to understand the nature of existence. Billboards in European cities celebrate teenagers in underwear. The Tibetan billboard is the *mani* wall, mantras carved into stone, prayers for the well being of all sentient beings."

The essence of the Buddhist path, Matthieu explained, is distilled in the Four Noble Truths. All life is suffering. By this the Buddha did not mean that all life was negation, but only that terrible things happen. Evil was not exceptional but part of the existing order of things, a consequence of human actions or karma. The cause of suffering was ignorance. By ignorance the Buddha did not mean stupidity. He meant the tendency of human beings to cling to the cruel illusion of their own permanence and centrality, their isolation and separation from the stream of universal existence. The third of the Noble Truths was the revelation that ignorance could be overcome, and the fourth and most essential was the delineation of a contemplative practice that if followed promised an end to suffering and a true liberation and transformation of the human heart. The goal was not to escape the world, but to escape being enslaved by it. The purpose of practice was not the elimination of self, but the annihilation of ignorance, and the unmasking of the true Buddha nature, which like a buried jewel shines bright within every human being, waiting to be revealed. The Buddha's transmission, in short, offered nothing less than a road map to enlightenment.

Over the course of nearly a month Matthieu and Sherab led me on a remarkable pilgrimage that ultimately took us to the flank of Everest. Our goal was not the mountain, but the home of a simple Buddhist nun by the name of Tsetsam Ani. Sherab explained that as a young woman she had been very beautiful, but devoted to the dharma, and with no interest in marriage. Pursued nevertheless by a wealthy merchant who had the power to demand of her family betrothal, she escaped by climbing down a cliffside latrine and eventually made her way on foot across the Himalaya into Tibet, where she took her vows. When she returned to her Nepali home in the Khumbu Valley, she entered lifelong retreat. For forty-five years she had not left the confines of a single small room. She had some human contact. Food was brought each day, and now that she was elderly Sherab as a physician examined her from time to time. But she had fundamentally dedicated her life to contemplative practice and solitude. She was the hero of heroes, a true Bodhisattva, the wisdom hero, the realized being who had found enlightenment and yet remained in the realm of samsara, of suffering and ignorance, to assist all sentient beings achieve their own liberation.

Approaching the shuttered window of her tiny room, I half expected to be met by a mad woman. Instead the wooden door opened to reveal the happiest of eyes, sparkling with light and laughter. Her hair was speckled with grey and cut short. Her body was slight but strong, and only when her hands came together in ritual greeting did I realize how old she indeed was. She offered us sweets, and then immediately took Matthieu to task for the elaborate, baroque, and quite unnecessary rituals of the monastic life. She had distilled her entire religious practice into a single mantra, *Om Mani Padme Hum,* six syllables representing the six realms that must be passed before the whole of samsara is emptied and complete purity is embraced through the heart essence of the Buddha. In reciting this one prayer every waking moment for forty-five years she had dedicated herself to the spreading of compassion and loving kindness. With each breath she had moved that much closer to her goal, which was not a place but a state of mind, not a destination but a path of salvation and liberation.

We stayed with Tsetsam Ani for perhaps an hour and then left her to her devotions. As we moved away from the village we happened to pass some climbers making their way toward Everest base camp. Most of us would find it inconceivable to do what this gentle woman had done; some would call it a waste of a human life. Most Tibetan Buddhists find it equally incomprehensible that one would choose to walk to heights where the air is so thin that consciousness is obliterated. To enter a death zone deliberately, to risk losing the opportunity of personal transformation and escape from the realm of samsara, merely to climb a mountain, is for them a fool's folly, the actual waste of a precious incarnation.

The Buddhists spend their time getting prepared for a moment that we spend most of our lives pretending does not exist, which is death. We dwell in a whirlwind of activity, racing against time, defining success by measures of the material world, wealth and achievements, credentials of one sort or another. This to the Buddhists is the essence of ignorance. They remind us that all life grows old and that all possessions decay. Every moment is precious and we all have a choice, to continue on the spinning carousel of delusion, or to step off into a new realm of spiritual possibilities. They offer an alternative that is not a dogma but a path, long and difficult but in so many ways irresistible.

The Buddhists speak not of sin and judgment, of good and evil, but only of ignorance and suffering, with all emphasis being on compassion. To take refuge in the

Buddha demands no act of blind faith, and certainly implies no mandate to go out and persuade the rest of the world to think as you think. At its core it is simply a wisdom philosophy, a set of contemplative practices, a spiritual path informed by 2,500 years of empirical observation and deduction that, if followed, offers the certain promise of a transformation of the human heart. Finding serenity through the dharma is the experimental proof that validates the Buddhist science of the mind, just as a falling apple proves to us the existence of gravity. It may be hard to understand what all of this means, but it exists for the Tibetans. Many Tibetans do not believe that we went to the moon, but we did. We may not believe that they achieve enlightenment in this lifetime, but they do.

In the Diamond Sutra, the Buddha cautions that the world is fleeting, like a candle in the wind, a phantom, a dream, the light of stars fading with the dawn. It is upon this insight that Tibetans measure their past and chart their future. They leave the rest of the world to ask how we possibly could have allowed such a blast of sorrow to sweep through their land, and why to this day we continue to tolerate the wrath of China, even as it pursues the dismantling of Tibetan culture and the violation of a people and a nation that has truly given so much to humanity.

CRUEL AND COMPLEX as the Chinese domination of Tibet has been, it is fundamentally a story of power and presumption, the economic and military capability of one people to impose its will on another, and the assertion of superiority of knowledge and culture that such an imposition implies. This essential dynamic also drives the cult of progress that is the modern development paradigm. The motivations may in some instances be more benign, though certainly the Chinese government believes strongly in the righteousness of its policies in Tibet, but the consequences can be equally devastating for the peoples and cultures whose lives the international community has elected to change and improve.

In the Kaisut desert of northern Kenya, drought is not a cruel anomaly but a regular feature of climate. Surviving drought is the key adaptive imperative of all the pastoral nomads, tribal peoples such as the Rendille, Samburu, Ariaal, Boran, and Gabra. To guarantee the continuity of the clan it is vital to maintain herds of camels and cattle large enough so that at least some animals will survive an extreme period of desiccation and provide the essential capital from which to rebuild the wealth of the family. To a great extent this liability and obligation determines the structure of the society; it makes the people who they are. To maintain large herds it is useful for a patriarch to have a large number of children, and thus these societies typically are polygamous. But with men taking multiple wives, there is the challenge of dealing with virile young men of marriageable age who may not have partners to marry. The elders solve this problem essentially by getting rid of the young men, dispatching them for a period of ten years to remote encampments where they are charged with the duty of protecting the herds from enemy raiders. To make this separation from the social space of the community desirable, it is enveloped in prestige. The greatest event of a young man's life, a ritual for which he trains for months, is his public circumcision, the moment when he enters the privileged world of the warrior. The ceremony is held only once every fourteen years, and those who endure it together are bonded for life. Should a lad flinch as the nine slits are made to the foreskin, he will shame his clan forever. But few fail, for the honour is immense.

Transformed physically, socially, and spiritually, the warriors move to the desert, where they live together on a diet of herbs gathered in the shade of frail acacia trees, mixed with milk and blood drawn each night from the jugular of a heifer. Still, there remains the problem of the human libido. To resolve this dilemma the warriors are allowed to return periodically to the community, provided they go nowhere near the married women. They are, however, permitted to approach unmarried maidens. Premarital sexual liaisons are open and tolerated, up until the moment the young woman is betrothed to an elder, at which time the relationship must cease. But the warrior is encouraged and indeed expected to attend the wedding of his former lover and publicly mock the virility of the old man who has taken his place at his lover's side. A single adaptive challenge, surviving drought, reverberates through the entire culture, defining for these nomadic tribes what it means to be human.

In the 1970s and 1980s a series of catastrophic droughts, along with famine caused by ethnic conflict and war in neighbouring Ethiopia and Somalia, drew international attention to the Kaisut and adjacent regions of sub-Saharan Africa. The development community suggested that the degradation of the Sahel and the impoverishment of the people was a consequence of overgrazing, which in academic vernacular came to be known as the "tragedy of the commons." As long as people did not own land, individual greed would inevitably triumph over community interests. The solution was privatization and the imposition of a land management plan imported wholesale from the American West. In 1976, the United Nations launched a multimillion-dollar initiative to encourage the tribes to settle and enter a cash economy, reducing the size of their herds by selling stock. This external prescription, which echoed British colonial efforts since the 1920s to convert the tribes to sedentary life, ignored the obvious fact that for hundreds of years the very survival of the nomads had been dependent on them looking after the land. The desert was their home. Using animals to convert the grasses and scrub vegetation to protein was the most efficient use of the land and the only way to live in the desert. Mediating the process, securing the rights and well-being of every individual to the fate of the collective, were complex ties of kinship, relationships too subtle to be perceived readily by outsiders. The genius of the nomads was their very ability to survive in the desert.

The problems began when a people born to move were obliged to settle down. Watering holes grew into relief camps and these in time into small towns, all oases of dependency. Those who sold their animals became wards of international aid agencies, which distributed maize, Iowa corn for the most part, that had to be boiled to be edible, and thus the last of the trees were cut to make charcoal. Those lucky enough to have the means dispatched their eldest sons to be educated at mission stations, where they came into the orbit of the church.

When I travelled through the Kaisut in 1998 I visited a mission at Korr, a refugee settlement, and met a wonderful man, Father George, an Italian priest who had established the food relief operation in 1975. At that time Korr was just a seasonal camp, a source of water visited by small bands of nomadic Rendille herders. When I was there, only a generation later, there was a population of 16,000, 170 hand-dug wells, and 2,500 houses, all roofed in cardboard, burlap, and metal sheets bearing the names of international aid organizations. Father George was his own harshest critic. "Schooling," he told me, "has not changed the people for the better. This is the pain in my heart. Those educated want nothing to do with their animals. They just want to leave. Education should not be a reason to go away. It's an obligation to come back."

The problem is that few do. As Father George acknowledged, they acquire a modicum of literacy and certain basic skills, but in an atmosphere and with a pedagogy that teaches them to have contempt for their fathers and their traditions. They enter school as nomads, graduate as clerks, and drift south to the cities where the official unemployment rate is 25 percent and more than half of high school graduates are without work. Caught between worlds, unable to go back, and with no clear path forward, they scratch for a living in the streets of Nairobi and swell the sea of misery that surrounds the Kenyan capital.

"They must hold onto tradition," Father George told me. "Ultimately it is what will save them. It's all they have. They are Rendille and must stay Rendille."

BEFORE SHE DIED, anthropologist Margaret Mead spoke of her singular fear that, as we drift toward a more homogenous world, we are laying the foundations of a blandly amorphous and singularly generic modern culture that will have no rivals. The entire imagination of humanity, she feared, might be confined within the limits of a single intellectual and spiritual modality. Her nightmare was the possibility that we might wake up one day and not even remember what had been lost. Our species has been around for some 200,000 years. The Neolithic Revolution, which gave us agriculture, and with it surplus, hierarchy, specialization, and sedentary life, occurred only ten to twelve thousand years ago. Modern industrial society as we know it is scarcely 300 years old. This shallow history should not suggest to any of us that we have all the answers for all of the challenges that will confront us as a species in the coming millennia. The goal is not to freeze people in time. One cannot make a rainforest park of the mind. Cultures are not museum pieces; they are communities of real people with real needs. The question, as Hugh Brody has written, is not the traditional versus the modern, but the right of free peoples to choose the components of their lives. The point is not to deny access, but rather to ensure that all peoples are able to benefit from the genius of modernity on their own terms, and without that engagement demanding the death of their ethnicity.

It is perhaps useful to reflect on what we mean when we use the term *modernity*, or *the modern world*. All cultures are ethnocentric, fiercely loyal to their own interpretations of reality. Indeed, the names of many indigenous societies translate as "the people," the implication being that every other human is a non-person, a savage from beyond the realm of the civilized. The word *barbarian* derives from the Greek *barbarus*, meaning one who babbles. In the ancient world, if you did not speak Greek, you were a barbarian. The Aztec had the same notion. Anyone who could not speak Nahuatl was a non-human.

We too are culturally myopic and often forget that we represent not the absolute wave of history but merely a world view, and that modernity — whether you identify it by the monikers *westernization, globalization, capitalism, democracy,* or *free trade* — is but an expression of our cultural values. It is not some objective force removed from the constraints of culture. And it is certainly not the true and only pulse of history. It is merely a constellation of beliefs, convictions, economic paradigms that represent one way of doing things, of going about the complex process of organizing human activities. Our achievements to be sure have been stunning, our technological innovations dazzling. The development within the last century of a modern, scientific system of medicine alone represents one of the greatest episodes in human endeavour. Sever a limb in a car accident and you won't want to be taken to an herbalist.

But these accomplishments do not make the Western paradigm exceptional or suggest in any way that it has or ought to have a monopoly on the path to the future. An anthropologist from a distant planet landing in the United States would see many wondrous things. But he or she or it would also encounter a culture that reveres marriage, yet allows half of its marriages to end in divorce; that admires its elderly, yet has grandparents living with grandchildren in only 6 percent of its households; that loves its children, yet embraces a slogan — "twenty-four/seven" — that implies total devotion to the workplace at the expense of family. By the age of eighteen, the average American youth has spent two years watching television. One in five Americans is clinically obese and 60 percent are overweight, in part because 20 percent of all meals are consumed in automobiles and a third of children eat fast food every day. The country manufactures 200 million tons of industrial chemicals each year, while its people consume two-thirds of the world's production of antidepressant drugs.

The four hundred most prosperous Americans control more wealth than 2.5 billion people in the poorest eighty-one nations with whom they share the planet. The nation spends more money on armaments and war than the collective military budgets of its seventeen closest rivals. The state of California spends more money on prisons than on universities. Technological wizardry is balanced by the embrace of an economic model of production and consumption that compromises the life supports of the planet. *Extreme* would be one word for a civilization that contaminates with its waste the air, water, and soil; that drives plants and animals to extinction on a scale not seen on earth since the disappearance of the dinosaurs; that dams the rivers, tears down the ancient forests, empties the seas of fish, and does little to curtail industrial processes that threaten to transform the chemistry and physics of the atmosphere.

Our way of life, inspired in so many ways, is not the paragon of humanity's potential. Once we look through the anthropological lens and see, perhaps for the first time, that all cultures have unique attributes that reflect choices made over generations, it becomes absolutely clear that there is no universal progression in the lives and destiny of human beings. Were societies to be ranked on the basis of technological prowess, the Western scientific experiment, radiant and brilliant, would no doubt come out on top. But if the criteria of excellence shifted, for example to the capacity to thrive in a truly sustainable manner, with a true reverence and appreciation for the earth, the Western paradigm would fail. If the imperatives driving the highest aspirations of our species were to be the power of faith, the reach of spiritual intuition, the philosophical generosity to recognize the varieties of religious longing, then our dogmatic conclusions would again be found wanting.

When we project modernity, as we define it, as the inevitable destiny of all human societies, we are being disingenuous in the extreme. Indeed, the Western model of development has failed in so many places in good measure because it has been based on the false promise that people who follow its prescriptive dictates will in time achieve the material prosperity enjoyed by a handful of nations of the West. Even were this possible, it is not at all clear that it would be desirable. To raise consumption of energy and materials throughout the world to Western levels, given current population projections, would require the resources of four planet Earths by the year 2100. To do so with the one world we have would imply so severely compromising the biosphere that the earth would be unrecognizable. Given the values that drive most decisions in the international community, this is not about to happen. In reality, development for the vast majority of the peoples of the world has been a process in which the individual is torn from his past, propelled into an uncertain future, only to secure a place on the bottom rung of an economic ladder that goes nowhere.

Consider the key indices of the development paradigm. An increase in life expectancy suggests a drop in infant mortality, but reveals nothing of the quality of the lives led by those who survive childhood. Globalization is celebrated with iconic intensity. But what does it really mean? In Bangladesh, garment workers are paid pennies to sew clothing that retails in the United States and Canada for tens of dollars. Eighty percent of the toys and sporting goods sold in America are produced in sweatshops in China, where millions work for wages as low as 12 cents an hour, 400,000 die prematurely each year due to air pollution, and 400 million people do not have access to potable water, so ruined are the rivers with industrial toxins. *The Washington Post* reports that in Lahore, Pakistan, one Muhammad Saeed earns $88 a month stitching shirts and jeans at a factory that supplies Gap and Eddie Bauer. He and his five family members share a single bed in a one-room home tucked away in a warren of alleys strewn with sewage and refuse. Earning three times the money that he made at his last job, he is the poster child of globalization.

Without doubt, images of comfort and wealth, of technological sophistication, have a magnetic allure. Any job in the city may seem better than back-breaking labour in sun-scorched fields. Entranced by the promise of the new, people throughout the world have in many instances voluntarily and in great earnest turned their backs on the old. The consequences, as we have seen in Kenya, can be profoundly disappointing. The fate of the vast majority of those who sever their ties with their traditions will not be to attain the prosperity of the West, but to join the legions of urban poor, trapped in squalor, struggling to survive. As cultures wither away, individuals remain, often shadows of their former selves, caught in time, unable to return to the past, yet denied any real possibility of securing a place in a world whose values they seek to emulate and whose wealth they long to acquire. This creates a dangerous and explosive situation, which is precisely why the plight of diverse cultures is not a simple matter of nostalgia or even of human rights alone, but a serious issue of geopolitical stability and survival.

Were I to distill a single message from these Massey Lectures it would be that culture is not trivial. It is not decoration or artifice, the songs we sing or even the prayers we chant. It is a blanket of comfort that gives meaning to lives. It is a body of knowledge that allows the individual to make sense out of the infinite sensations of consciousness, to find meaning and order in a universe that ultimately has neither. Culture is a body of laws and traditions, a moral and ethical code that insulates a people from the barbaric heart that history suggests lies just beneath the surface of all human societies and indeed all human beings. Culture alone allows us to reach, as Abraham Lincoln said, for the better angels of our nature.

If you want to know what happens when the constraints of culture and civilization are lost, merely look around the world and consider the history of the last century. Anthropology suggests that when peoples and cultures are squeezed, extreme ideologies often emerge, inspired by strange and unexpected beliefs. These *revitalization movements*, a terrible and misleading academic term, may be benign. In Jamaica, 300 years of colonialism followed by the economic doldrums of independence sent scores of young men to the shanties of Trenchtown where, infused with perhaps too much marijuana, the Rastafarians cast Haile Selassie, a minor African despot, as the Lion of Judah. This was a peculiar notion to be sure, but ultimately harmless.

More typically, such movements prove deadly both to their adherents and to those they engage. In China at the turn of the century, the Boxer Rebellion did not seek just the end of the opium trade or the expulsion of foreigners. The Boxers rose in response to the humiliation of an ancient nation, long the centre of the known world, reduced within a generation to servitude by unknown barbarians at the gate. It was not enough to murder the missionaries. In a raw, atavistic gesture, their bodies were dismembered, their heads displayed on pikes.

In Cambodia, Pol Pot, humiliated at home by the French and in Paris when he went abroad to study, created a fantasy of a renewed Khmer empire, a nation purged of all things Western, save the essential ideology that rationalized murder. Thus, while the great twelfth-century temples of Angkor were spared destruction during the civil war, all those who wore reading glasses or had the soft hands of scholars, poets, merchants, and priests were liquidated in the killing fields.

In the Democratic Republic of Congo, systematic rape is today codified as a weapon of terror, the only coherent strategy of war, while in Uganda militias of orphaned youth ravage and pillage in the name of Christ. In Liberia naked children high on drugs went into battle as the Butt Naked Battalion, a cult led by a messianic warlord, Joshua Milton Blahyi, who convinced them that his satanic powers would make them invincible. In fourteen years of civil war they murdered, raped, and cannibalized thousands. With the peace, General Butt Naked, as Blahyi was known, reinvented himself as an evangelical preacher and set out in search of converts and redemption on the streets of Monrovia, the Liberian capital, where he lives today.

In Nepal rural farmers spout rhetoric not heard since the death of Stalin. In Peru the Shining Path turned to Mao. Had they invoked instead Túpac Amaru, the eighteenth-century indigenous rebel, scion of the Inca, and had they been able to curb their reflexive disdain for the very indigenous people they claimed to represent, they might well have set the nation aflame, as was their intent. Lima, a city of 400,000 in 1940, is today home to 9 million, and for the majority it is a sea of poverty in a sun-scorched desert.

Torn between worlds, al Qaeda followers invoke a feudal past that never was in order to rationalize their own humiliation and hatred. They are a cancer within the culture of Islam, neither fully of the faith nor totally apart from it. Like any malignant growth they must be severed from the body and destroyed. At the same time, we must strive to understand the roots of this and other such movements, for the chaotic conditions of disenfranchisement are found amongst disaffected populations throughout the world.

We live in an age of disintegration. At the beginning of the twentieth century there were 60 nation-states. Today there are 190, most of them poor and highly unstable. The real story lies in the cities. Throughout the world, urbanization, with all of its promises, has drawn people by the millions into squalor. The populations of Mexico City and São Paulo are unknown, probably immeasurable. In Asia there are cities of ten million people that most of us in the West cannot name. In the next twenty years the world's population will grow from 6 to 8 billion, and 97 percent of this increase will occur in nations where the average individual income is less than $2 a day.

The nation-state, as Harvard sociologist Daniel Bell wrote, has become too small for the big problems of the world and too big for the little problems of the world. Outside of the major industrial nations, globalization has not brought integration and harmony, but rather a firestorm of change that has swept away languages and cultures, ancient skills and visionary wisdom.

This does not have to happen. To acknowledge the wonder of other cultures is not to denigrate our way of life but rather to recognize with some humility that other peoples, flawed as they too may be, nevertheless contribute to our collective heritage, the human repertoire of ideas, beliefs, and adaptations that have historically allowed us as a species to thrive. To appreciate this truth is to sense viscerally the tragedy inherent in the loss of a language or the assimilation of a people. To lose a culture is to lose something of our selves.

SOME YEARS AGO I found myself in Borneo sitting by a fire with an old friend, Asik Nyelik, headman of the Ubong River Penan. The rains that had pounded the forest all day had finally stopped. The head of a barking deer that Asik had killed roasted in the coals at our feet. The clouds opened and through the branches of the canopy the light of a full moon suddenly illuminated our camp. Asik looked up at the moon and casually asked if it was true that people had gone there, only to return with baskets of rocks. If that was all they had found, why had they bothered to go? How long had it taken and what kind of transport had they had? It was difficult to explain to a man who kindled fire with flint a space program that had consumed the wealth of nations and at a cost of nearly a trillion dollars placed twelve men on the moon. Or that after travelling several billion miles through space they had indeed brought back only rocks and lunar dust, 828 pounds altogether.

But the answer to Asik's question was in a sense obvious. We did not go into space to secure wealth. We went because we could, and we were curious, and we returned not with treasure but with something infinitely more valuable, a new vision of life itself. The seminal moment came on Christmas Eve, 1968, when Apollo 8 emerged from the dark side of the moon to see rising over its surface a small and fragile planet, floating in the velvet void of space. Not a sunrise, or the shadow of a moon, but Earth itself ascendant. This image more than any amount of scientific data showed us that our planet is a finite place, a single interactive sphere of life, a living organism composed of air, water, wind, and soil. Story Musgrave, the first physician to walk in space, once told me that to have experienced that vision, a sight made possible only by the brilliance of scientific technology, and then to recall the callous and unconscious manner in which we treat our only home, was to know the purest sensation of horror. But also, he added, the excitement and anticipation of a new beginning, because peoples and nations would have to change their ways.

And they did. Just forty years ago simply getting people to stop throwing garbage out of car windows was considered a great environmental victory. Rachel Carson was a lone voice in the wild. A mere decade ago scientists who warned of the gravity of global warming were dismissed as radicals. Today, it is those who question the significance of climate change who occupy the lunatic fringe. When I was a graduate student the words *biosphere* and *biodiversity* were exotic terms, familiar only to a handful of scientists. Today they are part of the vocabulary of schoolchildren. The biodiversity crisis, marked by the extinction of over a million life forms in the past three decades alone, has emerged as one of the central issues of our times. Though solutions to the major environmental challenges may remain elusive, no government on earth can ignore the magnitude of the threat or the urgency of the dilemma. This represents a reorientation of human priorities that is both historic in its significance and profoundly hopeful in its promise.

A similar shift is occurring, and not a minute too soon, in the way that people view and value culture. In many ways Canada is leading the way, not only as a model of a successful multicultural country, but as a nation-state prepared to acknowledge past mistakes and seek appropriate means of restitution even as it charts a way forward as a pluralistic society. I am reminded of this every time I travel in the Arctic, especially to Nunavut, the new territory, a homeland roughly the size of western Europe now under the administrative control of 26,000 Inuit people. With the possible exception of Colombia, I cannot think of another nation-state that has made such a choice. Nunavut's very existence is a powerful statement to the world that Canada recognizes that unique ethnicities, indigenous peoples, First Nations, do not stand in the way of a country's destiny; rather they contribute to it, if given a chance. Their cultural survival does not undermine the nation-state; it serves to enrich it, if the state is willing to embrace diversity. These cultures do not represent failed attempts at modernity, marginal peoples who somehow missed the technological train of history. On the contrary, these peoples, with their dreams and prayers, their myths and memories, teach us that there are indeed other ways of being, alternative visions of life, birth, death, and creation itself. When a nation-state is prepared to acknowledge this, then surely there is hope for all the peoples of the world.

The power of this idea grows even stronger when you consider how far we have come as Canadians in redefining this relationship. For the Inuit, in particular, the original clash of cultures was traumatic in the extreme. When the British first arrived in the Arctic they took the Inuit to be savages; the Inuit took the British to be gods. Both were wrong, but one did more to honour the human race. The British failed to understand that there was no better measure of genius than the ability to survive in the Arctic environment with a technology that was limited to what you could carve from ivory and bone, antler, soapstone and slate. The runners of sleds were originally made from fish, three Arctic char laid in a row, wrapped in caribou hide and frozen. The Inuit did not fear the cold, they took advantage of it.

European expeditions that mimicked their ways achieved great feats of exploration. Those that failed to do so suffered terrible deaths. When Lord Franklin's men were found frozen to death at Starvation Cove on the Adelaide peninsula, the young sailors were stiff in the leather traces of a sled made of iron and oak that weighed 650 pounds. On it was an 800-pound dory loaded with all the personal effects of British Naval officers, including silver dinner plates and even a copy of the novel *The Vicar of Wakefield*. This they somehow expected to drag across the ice and through the immense boreal forests of the north, all with the hope of encountering another ship, or perhaps an outpost of the Hudson's Bay Company.

The Inuit, by contrast, moved lightly on the land. I once spent a few days with several families from Arctic Bay in a hunting camp at Cape Crauford at the tip of Baffin Island. Each summer in June, in one of the most epic animal migrations on earth, 17 million marine mammals return to the Arctic, passing through the open waters of Lancaster Sound. Admiralty Inlet, which clefts the northern shore of Baffin Island, remains icebound, and the hunters travel along the floe edge, where the ice meets the sea, and listen as the breath of whales mingles with the wind. One day, or perhaps it was night, for the sun in June never fades, Olayuk Narqitarvik told me a remarkable story. During the 1940s and 1950s, a dark period in the history of the country, the Canadian government, in order to establish sovereignty in the Arctic, essentially forced the Inuit into settlements, in some cases moving entire populations hundreds of kilometres from their homes. There was one old man who refused to go. Fearful for his life, his family took away all of his tools and weapons, thinking this would oblige him to leave the land. Instead, in the midst of a winter storm, he stepped out of their igloo, defecated, and honed the feces into a frozen blade, which he sharpened with a spray of saliva. With this knife, forged by the cold from human waste, he killed a dog. Using its rib cage as a sled and its hide to harness another dog, he disappeared into the darkness. This story may well be apocryphal, though I did find a reference to just such an implement in the Arctic journals of the Danish explorer Peter Freuchen. But true or not, it is a wonderful symbol of the ingenuity and resilience of the Inuit people, traits of culture that have allowed them to survive.

I was reminded of this on a more recent trip to the Arctic, as Canadian filmmaker Andy Gregg and I joined Theo Ikummaq and John Arnatsiaq and a party of hunters from Igloolik as they set out on the sea ice in search of polar bear. We were travelling perhaps 150 kilometres offshore, and with the wind chill the temperature hovered around minus 50 degrees Celsius. A snowmobile pulling a fully loaded *kamotik* hit a piece of rogue ice, spun out of control, and the momentum of the sled carried it up and over both driver and machine. One of the skis twisted like a pretzel, the other was torn completely in half. I watched in astonishment as Theo and John pounded out the metal, blasted four holes into it with rifles at close range, improvised clamps from a scrap of iron, scavenged a splint from a hockey stick, and had the entire works bound back together in twenty minutes. We pushed on into the night, and it was only days later that the driver casually mentioned that in the accident he had broken his foot.

Theo and John grew up together, and their lives in many ways encapsulate the story of the Inuit in the twentieth century. Igloolik, today the cultural heart of Nunavut, historically had remarkably little contact with the outside world. William Parry, with two ships of the British Navy, wintered in the ice off shore in 1821–22. In 1867 and again in 1868 the American explorer Charles Francis Hall passed through as he searched for survivors of the Franklin Expedition. A French-Canadian prospector, Alfred Tremblay, visited briefly in 1913, as did Peter Freuchen in 1921 as part of Knud Rasmussen's Fifth Thule Expedition. But that was the limit of the European encounter.

The Arctic formally passed from British to Canadian rule in 1880, but the first sustained contact at Igloolik did not occur until the arrival of Catholic missionaries in the 1930s. Their immediate goal was the destruction of the power and authority of the shaman, the cultural pivot, the heart of the Inuit relationship to the universe. To facilitate assimilation, they discouraged the use of traditional names, songs, and the language itself. As always, trading goods proved seductive, drawing the people toward the mission and away from the land, a process encouraged by government authorities whose presence was well established by the 1950s. A distemper epidemic allowed the authorities to rationalize the wholesale slaughter of Inuit dogs. The introduction of the snowmobile in the early 1960s increased dependence on the cash economy. Family allowance payments were made contingent on the children's attending school, creating another incentive to settle. The government conducted a census and because Inuktitut names were so difficult to transcribe, they identified each Inuk by a number, issuing identification tags, and eventually conducting Operation Surname, a bizarre effort to assign last names to individuals who never had them. More than a few Inuit dogs were recorded as Canadian citizens. A final blow came in the 1950s when the government, battling a tuberculosis outbreak, forcibly evacuated every Inuk to a hospital ship to be screened. Those who tested positive, roughly one in five, immediately were shipped south for treatment, many never to return. The psychological impacts on both those evacuated and those left behind were profound, and not dissimilar to what families endured when their children were forcibly removed from the home to be educated. At the ages of six and eight Theo and John were sent south 800 kilometres to a residential school at Chesterfield Inlet where, forbidden to speak their own language, and in the case of Theo violated by a priest, they remained for seven years.

When finally they were allowed to return home, their families took them immediately onto the land in what Theo today describes as a rescue mission. Over a series of years, he recalls, "They turned us back into Inuit men."

The culmination of his rebirth was an epic journey by dogsled, 1,800 kilometres from Igloolik across Baffin Island, north along the shore of Ellesmere Island and across Smith Sound to Greenland. Theo thought he might have relatives living in the small Inuit community of Qaanaaq, the most northern settlement in the world. As it turned out he did, all descendants of legendary shaman Qitdlarssuaq and a small band of six families who had migrated north in the 1850s, taking two full years to reach Greenland. Theo had done the journey in two months. Andy and I invited him to return with us, on a charter flight of a mere six hours. Almost immediately the plane crossed over the Baffin Island we could see from the expression on Theo's face that something was wrong. It was April and our flight path was taking us 12 degrees south of the North Pole. The sea ice was not there. Smith Sound, which Theo had crossed with his sled dogs, was open water. He stared out the plane window in disbelief. A tear grew in his eye as he said to no one in particular, "The ice should be frozen by October. This year it didn't come in until February. There were robins in Igloolik. We don't even have a word for them birds."

The Inuit are a people of the ice. As hunters they depend on it for their survival even as it inspires the very essence of their character and culture. Gretel Ehrlich, who lived eight years among the Polar Eskimo in Greenland, suggests that it is the nature of ice, the way it moves, recedes, dissolves, and reforms with the seasons, that gives such flexibility to the Inuit heart and spirit. "They have no illusions of permanence," she explains. "There is no time for regret. Despair is a sin against the imagination. Their grocery store is out there on the land and this creates an emotional life that's so much bigger than that of those who live in cities. They deal with death every day. To live they must kill the things they most love. Blood on ice is not a sign of death but an affirmation of life. Eating meat becomes a sacramental experience."

Gretel was waiting for us in Qaanaaq when we landed. With her was Jens Danielsen, her mentor in the north, a great bear of a man with an enormous heart and immense skills as a hunter. Like Theo, Jens had made an epic journey with dogs, in his case retracing the route of Rasmussen's Fifth Thule Expedition all the way from Greenland across the top of Canada to distant Alaska. In the company of these two remarkable individuals, Jens and Theo, our plan was to spend a fortnight on the ice, establishing a hunting camp beyond the western shore of Qeqertarsuaq Island, roughly two days from Qaanaaq. To get there we would travel by dogsleds. Qaanaaq alone among all Inuit communities in the Arctic had long ago banned the use of snowmobiles. In their wisdom the people had recognized that keeping sled dogs was the fulcrum of their culture. Dogs loosened the shackles binding the families to the cash economy. They made limitless the length of any journey. They honed the skills of the hunter, who had to provide a constant supply of meat. They brought security to the night. If you were a master of dogs, you were, as Jens said, a master of your life.

After pounding at high speed over hundreds of kilometres in *kamatiks*, with the constant high-pitched whine of engines, it was pure joy to head out over spring ice at the slow but steady pace of a dog team. It was movement as dream, the poetry of silence as steel runners ran over soft snow. The land seemed to rise out of the horizon, and oddly enough I was reminded of the *Hokule'a* and the wayfinders and how Nainoa always described the canoe as the sacred centre that itself never moves, as the vessel waits for the islands to come out of the sea. Theo and Jens were themselves navigators, not only of the geography of their lands but of their own cultural survival and that of their people. It was impossible to get lost in the Arctic, Theo had told me a week earlier, during a fierce blizzard that obliterated the sky and that forced eight of us to huddle for three days in a plywood shelter of less than 3 square metres. As Theo cooked Arctic char, Jens recalled each of the twenty-one polar bears he had killed, as well as a dozen others that had nearly killed him. All you had to do was read the snow. The prevailing winds caused all the drifts, large and small, to point to the northwest. In the dark, even running at high speed, Theo simply dragged a foot on the ground to know where he was going.

As it turned out the dogs were of limited value once we reached the island of Qeqertarsuaq. There were great open leads in the ice, and we were obliged to hunt by boat. Jens was stunned. He had never seen open water in April. In his language the word *sila* means both weather and consciousness. Weather brings animals or leads them away, allowing people to survive or causing them to die. The ice, Jens explained, used to form in September and remain solid until July. Now it comes in November and is gone by March. The hunting season has been cut in half in a single generation. Gretel told me of a trip she and Jens had made the previous summer. They were hunting narwhal and it rained every day. They had stood one afternoon alone on a headland, looking out to sea. "This is not our weather," Jens had said. "Where does it come from? I don't understand."

This then is the tragedy and perhaps the inspiration of the Arctic. A people that have endured so much — epidemic disease, the humiliation and violence of the residential schools, the culture of poverty inherent in the welfare system, drug and alcohol exposure leading to suicide rates six times that of southern Canada — now on the very eve of their emergence as a culture reborn politically, socially, and psychologically — find themselves confronted by a force beyond their capacity to resist. The ice is melting, and with it quite possibly a way of life.

THE HOPE LIES IN THE severity of the crisis. This past year for the first time in human history we became a predominantly urban species. In the year 1820 only London had a population of more than a million. Today there are 414 cities of such size or larger, and within 35 years demographers predict there will be more than 1,000, many following the pattern of places like Lagos, capital of Nigeria, which in 1955 had a population of 470,000 and by 2015 is projected to be home to over 16 million. Cloistered and insulated within urban space, in many cases living already in toxic conditions, city dwellers will not be the first to notice the consequences of global climate change. Nearly fifteen years ago I sat on the shore of Baffin Island with an Inuk elder, Ipeelie Koonoo, and watched as he carefully cleaned the carburetor of his

Ski-doo engine with the feather of an ivory gull. He spoke no English, and I did not know Inuktitut. But with Olayuk translating, Ipeelie told me then that the weather throughout the Arctic had become wilder, the sun hotter each year, and that for the first time Inuit were suffering from skin ailments, as he put it, caused by the sky.

The impacts of climate change are only beginning to be felt. Atmospheric levels of carbon dioxide are at their highest in 650,000 years. Oceans are becoming warmer and more acidic, and the population of zooplankton, the basis of the marine food chain, has dropped 73 percent since 1960. Natural habitats everywhere are under threat, the cloud forests of the Andes, the grasslands of the Asian steppe, the lowland rainforests of the Amazon, and the entire arid belt of the sub-Sahara from the Horn of Africa to the Atlantic shores of Mauritania. Half the coral reefs of the world either have died or are on the edge of collapse. The largest known insect infestation in the history of North America has destroyed millions of hectares of forest in the western United States, more than 130,000 square kilometres of lodgepole pine in British Columbia alone, and has now spread to Alberta to threaten the boreal forests of the Subarctic. In the Pacific and Indian oceans, island nations such as the Maldives, faced with the possibility of dramatic increases in sea level, have made contingency plans for the evacuation of their entire populations.

But arguably the greatest immediate threat is to be found in the mountain icefields that are the birthplaces of all the world's great rivers. On the Tibetan plateau, source of the Yellow River, the Mekong and Yangtze, the Brahmaputra, Salween, Sutlej, Indus, and Ganges, there has been no net accumulation of snow since at least 1950. These glaciers are not just retreating at the margins, they are melting from the surface down. Conservative estimates predict that 60 percent of China's glaciers will be gone by the end of this century. Half of humanity depends on these rivers. Five hundred million people in the Indian subcontinent alone turn to the Ganges for water; for 800 million Hindus it is the sacred Ganga Ma, holiest of rivers. During the dry season, fully 70 percent of the river's flow originates in the Gangotri glacier, which is receding at a rate of nearly 40 metres a year. If, as currently anticipated, the glacier completely disappears, the Ganges will become a seasonal river within our lifetimes. One shudders to anticipate the economic, political, and psychological consequences for India. In 2007 riots occurred when a few hundred pilgrims to the Amarnath Cave in Kashmir, located at 3,800 metres and one of the holiest of Hindu shrines, found that the phallus-shaped stalagmite of ice, for generations considered the sacred image of Lord Shiva, had melted.

Throughout the world mountain people who played no role in the creation of this crisis not only are seeing the impact of climate change on their lives, they are taking personal responsibility for the problem, often with a seriousness of intent that puts many of us to shame. Eighty percent of the fresh water that feeds the western coast of South America is derived from Andean glaciers. These are receding at such an obvious rate that the pilgrims to the Qoyllur Rit'i, believing the mountain gods to be angry, are no longer carrying ice from the Sinakara back to their communities, forgoing the very gesture of reciprocity that completes the sacred circle of the pilgrimage and allows for everyone to benefit from the grace of the divine. In the Sierra Nevada de Santa Marta in Colombia, the mamos observe each season the recession of the snow and icefields that for them are the literal heart of the world. They notice as well the disappearance of birds, amphibians, and butterflies, and the changing ecological character of the páramos, which are drying out. They have increased both their ritual and political activities, and have formally called on the Younger Brother to stop destroying the world. In Tanzania, the Chagga look up to a mountain that has lost more than 80 percent of its snowcap in a generation and ask what will happen to their fields and the very idea of Africa when Kilimanjaro no longer shines over the ancient continent.

THESE LECTURES SET OUT to ask "why ancient wisdom matters in the modern world." The phrase is somewhat flawed, implying if it does that these many remarkable peoples we have encountered are somehow vestigial, archaic voices stranded in time, having at best a vague advisory role to play in contemporary life. In truth, all the cultures I have referenced in these lectures — the Tibetans and the San, the Arhuacos, Wiwas and Kogi, the Kiowa, Barasana,

Makuna, Penan, Rendille, Tahltan, Gitxsan, Wet'suwet'en, Haida, Inuit, and all the peoples of Polynesia — are very much alive and fighting not only for their cultural survival but also to take part in a global dialogue that will define the future of life on earth. There are currently 1,500 languages gathered around the campfire of the Internet and the number is increasing by the week. Why should their voices be heard? There are scores of reasons, many of which I have alluded to at least implicitly in these lectures. But to sum up, two words will do. *Climate change*. There is no serious scientist alive who questions the severity and implications of this crisis, or the factors, decisions, and priorities that caused it to occur. It has come about because of the consequences of a particular world view. We have for three centuries now, as Thom Hartmann has written, consumed the ancient sunlight of the world. Our economic models are projections and arrows when they should be circles. To define perpetual growth on a finite planet as the sole measure of economic well-being is to engage in a form of slow collective suicide. To deny or exclude from the calculus of governance and economy the costs of violating the biological support systems of life is the logic of delusion.

These voices matter because they can still be heard to remind us that there are indeed alternatives, other ways of orienting human beings in social, spiritual, and ecological space. This is not to suggest naively that we abandon everything and attempt to mimic the ways of non-industrial societies, or that any culture be asked to forfeit its right to benefit from the genius of technology. It is rather to draw inspiration and comfort from the fact that the path we have taken is not the only one available, that our destiny therefore is not indelibly written in a set of choices that demonstrably and scientifically have proven not to be wise. By their very existence the diverse cultures of the world bear witness to the folly of those who say that we cannot change, as we all know we must, the fundamental manner in which we inhabit this planet. A climbing friend of mine once told me that the most amazing thing about summiting Everest was the realization that there was a place on earth where you could get up in the morning, tie on your boots, and under your own power walk in a single day into a zone where the air was so thin that humans could not survive. It was for him a revelation, a completely new perspective on the delicacy of this thin veil of atmosphere that allows life to exist on earth.

SOME YEARS AGO I travelled north from Timbuktu 1,000 kilometres into the Sahara to reach the ancient salt mine of Taoudenni. With a number of friends and colleagues, including Canadian photographer Chris Rainier, who had made the journey several times, I followed the route of the camel caravans that once defined commerce in West Africa. Until the Portuguese found a way to sail across the Bight of Benin and the Spaniards discovered and sacked the wealth of the Americas, two-thirds of Europe's gold moved overland from Ghana and the

African coast, fifty-two days by land across the Sahara to Morocco. Timbuktu, located in Mali, a day's travel north of the great bend in the Niger River, became the most important port on the great sea of sand that was the western desert. At a time when Paris and London were small medieval towns, Timbuktu was a thriving centre of 100,000 people, with 150 schools and universities, and some 25,000 students studying astronomy and mathematics, medicine, botany, philosophy, and religion. Rivalling Damascus, Baghdad, and Cairo, it was one of the great centres of Islamic culture and learning. The knowledge of the ancient Greeks survived to inspire the Renaissance only because it had been recorded and preserved by great Islamic scholars such as Avicenna, whose writings informed St. Thomas of the existence and philosophy of Aristotle. In Timbuktu I held in my hand a document embossed in gold and copied in the thirteenth century from an Avicenna manuscript written in the year 1037.

Today Timbuktu is a mostly forgettable place, dry and dusty, impossibly hot. In 1914, when the French took control of the city, they confiscated the ancient manuscripts, threatened the scholars with jail, and taught the children that their ancestors were not Arab or Berber, Tamashek or Tuareg, but Gaul. They also went after the salt trade, flooding the market with cheap sea salt from Marseilles, not out of economic rivalry but because of the symbolic importance of the traditional trade. The salt of Taoudenni was the gold of the Sahara, valued throughout West

Africa for its curative properties, and the culture of movement that grew up around its exchange defined the people. Until an Arab boy endured thirst and privation and crossed the desert, twenty days each way by camel, he could not marry or be considered a man. An old professor in Timbuktu, Salem Ould, described the journey as a test of strength, a physical and spiritual transformation that left the child a master of his senses. "In the endless ocean of sand," he said, "the young man realizes that there is something greater than himself, that he is but a small particle in the universe and that there is a higher being regulating the world. Thus is awakened a thirst for seeking. As they travel to the salt, they evoke the blessed names of God. The desert hones their devotion."

Our guide on the journey was a venerable elder, Baba Oumar, famous for having located a lost party of Legionnaires simply from their description over the radio of the scent and colour of the sand at their position. This story did not surprise Professor Ould. "They know the desert as a sailor knows the sea. When the wind blows they know what kind of wind. When a cloud gathers they can smell the rain. If thirsty they can sense the scent of water. With the camels there is a trust built on two thousand years. They know that they can close their eyes and the camels will lead them home. The Sahara has a science that is known to those who have crossed it for centuries."

We travelled north by Jeep, with Baba at times rather frantically pointing this way and that as our drivers raced over the flat pans of hard white ground. When we slowed to manoeuvre through soft sand, or take on water at a well, he took notice of the orientation of the dunes, the colour and texture of the sand, the patterns the wind made in the lee of desert plants. He carried an old French military compass, and from time to time lay spread-eagled taking a bearing. His true compass, however, was clearly within. Asked if he had ever been lost, he replied that orientation in the desert was a gift given to few and that if he ever was uncertain, he simply sat still and waited for a sign from Allah.

Two exceptional events unfolded over the next days. The mine itself was a biblical scene, mounds of excavated dirt piled for kilometres across the flat horizon of an ancient lakebed. Men stripped to the waist, skin cracked by salt, chipped away slabs of it with picks in the cave-like crevasses of underground pits. Our Tuareg companion Isa Mohammed took one look and said, "I would not bring my wife to this place." When I asked a group of men their nationalities, they replied, "There are no countries here."

On our last day at the mine, we met a man trapped in shame, beholden to debt, whose body though younger than mine had been broken by twenty-five years in the pits. He lived alone in a tiny room built of blocks of crude salt. His only possessions were a rusted oil drum and his tattered burnoose, a cloak of coarse wool with a hood that sheltered and shadowed his face. He had the eyes of a gazelle. In the entire 800-year history of the seasonal mine, he was the only person known to have spent a summer at the site. He survived by working at night, and slipping away before dawn to walk to a distant well, where he sat alone all day in temperatures that can melt sand. His debt, for which he had suffered so long, an obligation that had kept him from his family for two decades, was less than the cost of a dinner at an upscale restaurant in Toronto. Chris and I gave him the money, very discreetly. He simply said, *God be blessed*. As we left his hovel, a sandstorm blew across the mine, enveloping him like a veil. We never knew if the story was true, or if he had been beaten and robbed, or perchance actually had bought his way to freedom.

On our way back to Timbuktu, we came upon a caravan that we had passed on our way north. The freak thunderstorm that had pounded our camp with rain the night we arrived at Taoudenni had apparently swept the entire country. If the salt gets wet, it crumbles and loses all value, so the young men had been forced to stop in the desert to dry out the slabs in the sun. They lost three critical days, and by the time we ran into them they were down to their last quart or two of water. The six men were 150 kilometres from the nearest well, with a precious consignment of cargo and twenty or more camels that represented the entire wealth of their family. There was no sign of panic. As we pulled up I saw one of their mates with one camel shimmering as a mirage on the horizon to the east. Apparently they knew of a depression in the ground, some 25 kilometres distant, that if excavated to a sufficient depth might yield water.

Without food a body can live for weeks; without water, mere days. In the desert in the absence of water, delirium comes in an evening, and by morning one's mouth is open to the wind and sand, even as the eyes sink into another reality and strange chants echo from the lungs. The truck smugglers of the Sahara say that the good thing about brake fluid is that it keeps you away from the battery acid.

While we waited for their friend to return, Mohamed, the leader of the party, kindled a twig fire and with their last reserves of water offered us tea. It is said in the Sahara that if a stranger turns up at your tent, you will slaughter the last goat that provides the only milk for your children to feast your guest. One never knows when you will be that stranger turning up in the night, cold and hungry, thirsty and in need of shelter. As I watched Mohamed pour me a cup of tea, I thought to myself, these are the moments that allow us all to hope.

ANNOTATED BIBLIOGRAPHY

WHEN INITIALLY APPROACHED present the Massey Lectures I felt both deeply honoured and somewhat hesitant, for I had already published a short book, *Light at the Edge of the World* (Vancouver: Douglas & McIntyre, 2007; originally published as a book of photographs in 2001), which was both the ideal length for the Masseys, and a manifesto on the very issues and themes that attracted the CBC to my work. The proverbial well, I feared, might be dry. As it turned out, the challenge was ideal, for it obliged me to rethink old ideas, even as it provided a platform to explore much that was new in my experience.

I first wrote of language loss in a collection of essays, *The Clouded Leopard*, which Douglas & McIntyre published in 1998. This led to an article, "Vanishing Cultures," which appeared in *National Geographic* in August 1999. In 2000 I was invited to join the National Geographic Society as Explorer-in-Residence, with the mandate of helping the Society change the way the world viewed and valued culture. I had coined the term *ethnosphere* to inspire a new way of thinking about this extraordinary matrix of cultures that envelops the planet. But how could we actually make a difference? When biologists identify a region of critical importance in terms of biodiversity, they create a protected area. One cannot designate a rainforest park of the mind. As an anthropologist fully aware of the dynamic, ever-changing nature of culture, I had no interest in preserving anything. I just believed — as my mentor at Harvard, David Maybury-Lewis, once said — that all peoples ought to have the right to choose the components of their lives.

Recognizing that polemics are rarely persuasive, but with the hope that storytellers can change the world, I set out through the medium of film to take the global audience of *National Geographic*, literally hundreds of millions of people in 165 countries, to points in the ethnosphere where the beliefs, practices, and intuitions are so dazzling that one cannot help but come away with a new appreciation of the wonder of the human imagination made manifest in culture. My goal was not to document the exotic other, but rather to identify stories that had deep metaphorical resonance, something universal to tell us about the nature of being alive. We did not enter communities only as filmmakers and ethnographers; we were welcomed as collaborators, building on networks of relationships and friendships that often reached back for three decades or more. Our fundamental goal was to provide a platform for indigenous voices, even as our lens revealed inner horizons of thought, spirit, and adaptation that might inspire, in the words of Father Thomas Berry, entirely new dreams of the earth.

Many of the themes addressed in these lectures, as well as the experiences described, grew from these film projects — fifteen documentaries altogether, shot with various colleagues over the last seven years. In the series *Light at the Edge of the World*, I travelled to Hawaii, the Marquesas, Rapanui, and Tahiti to make *The Wayfinders*; to Greenland and Nunavut, to document the impact of climate change on the Inuit world in *Hunters of the Northern Ice*; to the Himalaya to reflect on Tibetan Buddhism and the *Science of the Mind*; and to Peru to examine the meaning and significance of notions of *Sacred Geography*. A second four films gave voice to the Arhuacos and the Elder Brothers in *The Magic Mountain*, celebrated the pastoral nomads of Mongolia in *The Windhorse*, explored the philosophy of the Aboriginal peoples of Australia in *Keepers of the Dream*, and visited the homeland of the Barasana in *Heart of the Amazon*. Other film projects led to the Sahara, the rain forests of Ecuador, the mountains of Oaxaca, the depths of the Grand Canyon and the homeland of Havasupai and Hualapai, Zuni, Hopi, Paiute, and Navajo. *Light at the Edge of the World*, the first four of these films, is available on DVD from Smithsonian Networks. The second four hours will be available in due course from National Geographic Channel.

CHAPTER ONE: SEASON OF THE BROWN HYENA

There is a large and growing literature on language loss and revitalization. Whereas estimates of species loss invariably provoke controversy and a range of opinions among biologists, linguists seem universally to recognize that half of the world's languages are at risk and may disappear within our lifetime. This academic consensus is itself haunting. Among recent books are: Andrew Dalby, *Language in Danger* (New York: Columbia University Press, 2003); David Crystal, *Language Death* (Cambridge: Cambridge University Press, 2000); K. David Harrison, *When Languages Die* (New York: Oxford University Press, 2007); Leanne Hinton and Ken Hale, eds., *The Green Book of Language Revitalization in Practice* (San Diego: Academic Press, 2001); Joshua Fishman, ed., *Can Threatened Languages Be Saved? Reversing Language Shift, Revisited: A 21st Century Perspective* (Clevedon, England: Multilingual Matters, 2001); Daniel Nettle and Suzanne Romaine, *Vanishing Voices* (New York: Oxford University Press, 2000); and Nicholas Ostler, *Empires of the Word: A Language History of the World* (New York: HarperCollins, 2005).

For catalogues of known languages, see: Raymond G. Gordon, Jr., ed., *Ethnologue: Languages of the World*, 15th ed. (Dallas: Summer Institute of Linguistics International, 2005), and David Crystal, *The Cambridge Encyclopedia of Language*, 2nd ed. (Cambridge: Cambridge University Press, 1997). For the links among language, landscape, knowledge, and environment, see: Luisa Maffi, ed., *On Biocultural Diversity* (Washington: Smithsonian Institute Press, 2001).

My understanding of the revelations of population genetics is deeply indebted to Spencer Wells, author of *Deep Ancestry: Inside the Genographic Project* (Washington, D.C.: National Geographic Books, 2006), and *The Journey of Man* (Princeton, N.J.: Princeton University Press, 2002), a wonderful book that grew out of a PBS film of the same name. I was first exposed to the Kalahari Bushman as a young student of Irven DeVore at Harvard in the early 1970s. No one at that time could have imagined that one day science would reveal the San to be the very trunk of our family tree, the oldest culture on earth. It would have seemed as preposterous as a claim to have identified the actual site of the Garden of Eden. But even this primordial point of origin has effectively been found, as indeed has been discovered with some precision the gate of departure of our species from Africa. The first to anticipate this extraordinary avenue of research was Spencer's mentor, Luigi Luca Cavalli-Sforza, author of *Genes, Peoples, and Languages* (Berkeley: University of California Press, 2001).

For the classic ethnographic works on the San, see: Richard B. Lee and Irven DeVore, eds., *Kalahari Hunter-Gatherers* (Cambridge, Mass.: Harvard University Press, 1976) and Richard B. Lee, *The !Kung San* (Cambridge: Cambridge University Press, 1979). For two engaging travel accounts see: Laurens van der Post, *The Lost World of the Kalahari* (New York: Harcourt Brace, 1977), and Rupert Isaacson, *The Healing Land* (New York: Grove Press, 2001). There are many fine illustrated books, but one of the best is Alf Wannenburgh's *The Bushmen* (Cape Town: Struik Publishers, 1979), photographed by Peter Johnson and Anthony Bannister.

Thomas Whiffen's book *The North-West Amazons: Notes on Some Months Spent Among Cannibal Tribes* was published in London by Constable in 1915. See also Eugenio Robuchon, *En el Putumayo y sus Afluentes* (Lima: Imprenta la Indústria, 1907), and Michael Taussig, *Shamanism, Colonialism, and the Wild Man* (Chicago: University of Chicago Press, 1987). For Steven Pinker's quotation, see "My Genome, My Self," *New York Times Magazine* (January 11, 2009). The two books by Carleton Coon, cited by Spencer Wells in *The Journey of Man*, are *The Origin of Races* (New York: Knopf, 1962) and *The Living Races of Man* (New York: Knopf, 1965). Lord Curzon is quoted in James Morris, *Farewell the Trumpets* (New York: Harcourt Brace Jovanovich, 1978), and Cecil Rhodes in Brian Moynahan's *The British Century* (New York: Random House, 1997).

Clayton Eshleman and his wife Caryl introduced me to the art of the Upper Paleolithic and generously shared with me their notes, which in turn were derived from Clayton's extraordinary book *Juniper Fuse: Upper Paleolithic Imagination and the Construction of the Underworld*

(Middletown, Conn.: Wesleyan University Press, 2003). For other sources on the Upper Paleolithic, see: Paul Bahn and Jean Vertut, *Journey Through the Ice Age* (London: Weidenfeld & Nicolson, 1997); Paul Bahn, *The Cambridge Illustrated History of Prehistoric Art* (Cambridge: Cambridge University Press, 1998); Dale Guthrie, *The Nature of Paleolithic Art* (Chicago: University of Chicago Press, 2005); André Leroi-Gourhan, *Treasures of Prehistoric Art* (New York: Harry N. Abrams, 1967); and Sigfried Giedion, *The Eternal Present: The Beginnings of Art*, Bollingen Series 35, 6.1 (New York: Pantheon Books, 1962). For Northrop Frye see: *Fearful Symmetry* (Princeton, N.J.: Princeton University Press, 1947; reprint, 1969) and *A Study of English Romanticism* (Chicago: University of Chicago Press, 1968).

CHAPTER TWO: THE WAYFINDERS

For the clash of cultures on the Marquesas, see: Edwin Ferdon, *Early Observations of Marquesan Culture, 1595–1813* (Tucson: University of Arizona Press, 1993); David Porter, *Journal of a Cruise Made to the Pacific Ocean*, 2 vols. (1822; reprint, Upper Saddle River, N.J.: The Gregg Press, 1970); Greg Dening, *Island and Beaches: Discourse on a Silent Land, Marquesas 1774–1880* (Honolulu: University Press of Hawaii, 1980); Greg Dening, ed., *The Marquesan Journal of Edward Robarts, 1797–1824*, Pacific History Series, no. 6 (Honolulu: University Press of Hawaii, 1974); E. S. Craighill Handy, *The Native Culture in the Marquesas*, Bernice P. Bishop Museum Bulletin 9 (Honolulu: Bernice P. Bishop Museum, 1923); Nicholas Thomas, *Marquesan Societies: Inequality and Political Transformation in Eastern Polynesia* (Oxford: Clarendon Press, 1990); and Willowdean Handy, *Forever the Land of Men: An Account of a Visit to the Marquesas Islands* (New York: Dodd, Mead & Co., 1965).

For the classic account of the sweet potato, see: D. E. Yen, *The Sweet Potato and Oceania: An Essay in Ethnobotany*, Bernice P. Bishop Museum Bulletin 236 (Honolulu: Bishop Museum Press, 1974). For the discovery of chicken bones at the pre-Columbian site of El Arenal, on the south coast of Chile, see: *Nature* 447, 620-621 (June 2007).

For the archaeology of the Pacific, the finest book is: Patrick Vinton Kirch, *On the Road of the Winds: An Archaeological History of the Pacific Islands before European Contact* (Berkeley: University of California Press, 2000). I find all of Kirch's work to be extraordinary. See two other books written by him — *The Evolution of the Polynesian Chiefdoms* (Cambridge: Cambridge University Press, 1984), and *The Lapita Peoples: Ancestors of the Oceanic World* (Malden, Mass.: Blackwell Publishers, 1997) — as well as the following co-authored works: Patrick Vinton Kirch and Jean-Louis Rallu, eds., *The Growth and Collapse of Pacific Island Societies: Archaeological and Demographic Perspectives* (Honolulu: University of Hawaii Press, 2007), and Patrick Vinton Kirch and Roger Green, *Hawaiki, Ancestral Polynesia: An Essay in Historical Anthropology* (Cambridge: Cambridge University Press, 2001).

For monographs and accounts of Polynesian navigation, see: David Lewis, *We, the Navigators: The Ancient Art of Landfinding in the Pacific* (Honolulu: University Press of Hawaii, 1972); David Lewis, *The Voyaging Stars: Secrets of the Pacific Island Navigators* (New York: W. W. Norton, 1978); Thomas Gladwin, *East is a Big Bird: Navigation and Logic on Puluwat Atoll* (Cambridge, Mass.: Harvard University Press, 1970); Stephen Thomas, *The Last Navigator* (New York: Henry Holt, 1987); Richard Feinberg, *Polynesian Seafaring and Navigation: Ocean Travel in Anutan Culture and Society* (Kent, Ohio: Kent State University Press, 1988); and Richard Feinberg, ed., *Seafaring in the Contemporary Pacific Islands: Studies in Continuity and Change* (DeKalb: Northern Illinois University Press, 1995).

Peter Buck's classic book is *Vikings of the Sunrise* (1938; reprint, Christchurch, N.Z.: Whitcombe & Tombs, 1954). Andrew Sharp presented his views in *Ancient Voyagers in Polynesia* (London: Penguin Books, 1957). His controversial notions of accidental drift prompted a fascinating gathering that yielded a collection of essays: Jack Golson, ed., *Polynesian Navigation: A Symposium on Andrew Sharp's Theory of Accidental Voyages* (Wellington, N.Z.: A. H. and A. W. Reed for the Polynesian Society, 1963).

Ben Finney, among the pioneering anthropologists at the University of Hawaii, wrote an account of the first experimental voyage of the sacred canoe: *Hokule'a: The Way to Tahiti* (New York: Dodd, Mead & Co., 1979). Much more about this complex and inspiring history can be found on the excellent website of the Polynesian Voyaging Society, http://pvs.kcc.hawaii.edu/aboutpvs.html.

Thor Heyerdahl expressed his misguided interpretations of the history of Rapa Nui and Polynesia in *Aku-Aku: The Secret of Easter Island*, appropriately published by Rand McNally (Chicago, 1958). His *Kon-Tiki: Across the Pacific in a Raft* (New York: Simon & Schuster, 1964), originally published in 1950, remains available as a mass-market paperback, and has appeared in sixty-five languages. Heyerdahl's ideas about Easter Island were thoroughly dismantled by Thomas Barthel, *The Eighth Land: The Polynesian Discovery and Settlement of Easter Island* (Honolulu: University Press of Hawaii, 1978). The best single archaeological source, based on more than thirty years of research by a remarkable team of Chilean scholars, has unfortunately yet to be translated into English: Patricia Vargas, Claudio Cristino, and Roberto Izaurieta, *1000 Años en Rapa Nui: Arqueología del Asentamiento* (Santiago: Editorial Universitaria, Universidad de Chile, 2006). Edmundo Edwards, who with Patricia and Claudio has excavated some 25,000 sites on the island, is about to publish his life's work. Although Edmundo and his colleagues conducted the pollen studies that unveiled the character of the endemic flora at the time of the arrival of the Polynesians, they reject the notion of a sudden collapse of island civilization that has been widely published and become almost a fable of the environmental movement. Their work suggests a culture in transition, with the Bird Man Cult representing not a sign of decadence and decay, but of reinvention and transformation that was interrupted crudely by the arrival of disease and other dire consequences of European contact.

Frances Widdowson and Albert Howard have written *Disrobing the Aboriginal Industry: The Deception Behind Indigenous Cultural Preservation* (Montreal: McGill-Queen's University Press, 2008). It is a book as bitter as it is uninformed. For fine biographies of Bronislaw

Malinowski and Franz Boas, see: Douglas Cole, *Franz Boas: The Early Years, 1858–1906* (Seattle: University of Washington Press, 1999), and Michael Young, *Malinowski: Odyssey of an Anthropologist, 1884–1920* (New Haven, Conn.: Yale University Press, 2004). Malinowski's classic work on Kula is: *Argonauts of the Western Pacific: An Account of Native Enterprise and Adventure in the Archipelagoes of Melanesian New Guinea* (Long Grove, Ill.: Waveland Press, 1984). First published in 1922, it is one of the great classics of anthropology. He wrote several other books, including *The Sexual Life of Savages in North-Western Melanesia: An Ethnographic Account of Courtship, Marriage, and Family Life among the Natives of the Trobriand Islands, British New Guinea* (London: George Routledge & Sons, 1932). For Malinowski's controversial field journals see: *A Diary in the Strict Sense of the Term* (1967; reprint, Stanford, Calif.: Stanford University Press, 1989). For an excellent book on the symbolic representations of the Kula see: Shirley Campbell, *The Art of Kula* (Oxford: Berg Press, 2002).

CHAPTER THREE: PEOPLES OF THE ANACONDA

For an engaging account of Orellana's encounter with the Amazon women see: Alex Shoumatoff, *In Southern Light* (New York: Simon & Schuster, 1986). Gaspar de Pinell was based at the Capuchin Mission at Sibundoy, at the headwaters of the Putumayo. His report *Excursión Apostólica por los Ríos Putumayo, San Miguel de Sucumbíos, Cuyabeno, Caquetá y Caguán* was published by Imprenta Nacional in Bogotá in 1928. *Green Hell: A Chronicle of Travel in the Forests of Eastern Bolivia,* by Julian Duguid, appeared in London in 1930, published by George Newnes Ltd. There were many such books. My own comments about tropical ecology and the fragility of the Amazon rainforest appeared in a collection of essays, *The Clouded Leopard* (Vancouver: Douglas & McIntyre, 1998). But we had all been reciting this by rote for more than twenty years.

For a sweeping and insightful survey of the Americas and the Amazon in particular before European contact see: Charles Mann, *1491: New*

Revelations of the Americas Before Columbus (New York: Vintage Books, 2006). For Charles Marie de la Condamine see: *Viaje a la América Meridional por el Río de las Amazonas* (1743; reprint, Barcelona: Editorial Alta Fulla, 1986). For the consequences of contact, see: Ronald Wright, *Stolen Continents: The Americas Through Indian Eyes Since 1492* (Boston: Houghton Mifflin, 1992). Paul Richards's classic book is *The Tropical Rain Forest: An Ecological Study* (New York: Cambridge University Press, 1952). For my own travels in the Andes and Northwest Amazon, the work with Tim Plowman on coca, and subsequent botanical explorations see: *One River: Explorations and Discoveries in the Amazon Rain Forest* (New York: Simon & Schuster, 1996).

For the dispute between Betty Meggers and Anna Roosevelt, see Charles Mann's excellent discussion in *1491* (cited above), as well as: Betty Meggers, *Amazonia: Man and Culture in a Counterfeit Paradise* (Arlington Heights, Ill.: AHM Publishing, 1971); Anna Roosevelt, *Moundbuilders of the Amazon: Geophysical Archaeology on Marajó Island, Brazil* (San Diego: Academic Press, 1991); and Anna Roosevelt, ed., *Amazonian Indians from Prehistory to the Present: Anthropological Perspectives* (Tucson: University of Arizona Press, 1994). For new thinking on the Amazon, see several publications of Bill Denevan: W. M. Denevan, *Cultivated Landscapes of Native Amazonia and the Andes* (New York: Oxford University Press, 2001); W. M. Denevan, ed., *The Native Population of the Americas in 1492* (Madison: University of Wisconsin Press, 1976); "The Native Population of Amazonia in 1492 Reconsidered," *Revista de Indias* 62, no. 227 (2003): 175–88; "The Pristine Myth: The Landscape of the Americas in 1492," *Annals of the Association of American Geographers* 82 (1992): 369–85; and "Stone vs. Metal Axes: The Ambiguity of Shifting Cultivation in Prehistoric Amazonia," *Journal of the Steward Anthropological Society* 20 (1992): 153–65. For Robert Carneiro on the efficiency of stone tools, see: "Tree Felling with the Stone Axe: An Experiment Carried Out Among the Yanomamö Indians of Southern Venezuela," in Carol Kramer, ed., *Ethnoarchaeology: Implications of Ethnography for Archaeology* (New York: Columbia University Press, 1979), 21–58. The classic account of the exchange of technology and agricultural products in the wake of the Conquest is: Alfred W.

Crosby, *The Columbian Exchange: Biological and Cultural Consequences of 1492* (Westport, Conn.: Greenwood Press, 1972). See also Crosby's *Ecological Imperialism: The Biological Expansion of Europe, 900–1900* (Cambridge: Cambridge University Press, 1986).

Over the past forty years a small but remarkable cadre of anthropologists, among them some of the most highly regarded ethnographers in the profession, have worked among the peoples of the Northwest Amazon of Colombia. The pioneer was Gerardo Reichel-Dolmatoff, a close friend and contemporary of my professor Richard Evans Schultes, who himself devoted the better part of twelve years to the study of the ethnobotany of the region. Schultes was the author of 10 books and 496 scientific papers. His most important books are *The Healing Forest: Medicinal and Toxic Plants of the Northwest Amazonia*, with Robert Raffauf (Portland, Ore.: Dioscorides Press, 1990); *The Botany and Chemistry of Hallucinogens*, with Albert Hofmann, 2nd ed., rev. and enl. (Springfield, Ill.: Charles C. Thomas, 1980); *Plants of the Gods*, with Albert Hofmann (New York: McGraw-Hill, 1979). There is a vast literature on ayahuasca, much of it written by Dennis McKenna. For the best single collection of papers, including contributions from Schultes, McKenna, Jean Langdon, Bronwen Gates, Luis Luna, and Anthony Henman, see: *América Indígena* 46(1) (1986): 5–256.

Reichel-Dolmatoff's books include: *Amazonian Cosmos: The Sexual and Religious Symbolism of the Tukano Indians* (Chicago: University of Chicago Press, 1971); *The Forest Within: The World-View of the Tukano Amazonian Indians* (Foxhole, England: Themis Books, 1996); *Rainforest Shamans: Essays on the Tukano Indians of the Northwest Amazon* (Foxhole, England: Themis Books, 1997); and *The Shaman and the Jaguar: A Study of Narcotic Drugs Among the Indians of Colombia* (Philadelphia: Temple University Press, 1975). See also: Jean Jackson, *The Fish People: Linguistic Exogamy and Tukanoan Identity in Northwest Amazonia* (Cambridge: Cambridge University Press, 1983); Kaj Arhem, *Makuna Social Organization* (Stockholm: Almqvist & Wiksell International, 1981); and Irving Goldman, *Cubeo Hehénewa Religious Thought*, posthumously edited and published by Peter Wilson (New York: Columbia University Press, 2004).

Stephen and Christine Hugh-Jones first lived among the Barasana in 1968. Both wrote seminal monographs. See: Christine Hugh-Jones, *From the Milk River: Spatial and Temporal Processes in Northwest Amazonia* (Cambridge: Cambridge University Press, 1979), and Stephen Hugh-Jones, *The Palm and the Pleiades: Initiation and Cosmology in Northwest Amazonia* (Cambridge: Cambridge University Press, 1979). Christine went on to study and practice medicine, but they have returned to the Río Piraparaná as a family on numerous occasions, and the Barasana and their neighbours clearly view them as revered elders. Both Graham Townsley, who directed *The Magic Mountain*, and Howard Reid, who directed *The Windhorse* and *Heart of the Amazon*, earned their doctorates under Stephen's direction at Cambridge.

Arguably the finest contemporary book on the beliefs and traditions of the Piraparaná was one written by the indigenous peoples of the river. See: Kaj Arhem, Luis Cayón, Gladys Angulo, and Maximiliano García, *Etnografía Makuna: Tradiciones, relatos y saberes de la Gente de Agua* (Bogotá: Instituto Colombiano de Antropología e Historia, 2004). Kaj Arhem and photographer Diego Samper collaborated on an exquisite illustrated book, *Makuna: Portrait of an Amazonian People* (Washington, D.C.: Smithsonian Institution Press, 1998). For the work of the Fundación Gaia Amazonas, see: Martin von Hildebrand, "Gaia and Culture: Reciprocity and Exchange in the Colombian Amazon," in Peter Bunyard, ed., *Gaia in Action, Science of the Living Earth* (Edinburgh: Floris Books, 1996). The website is: www.gaiaamazonas.org.

CHAPTER FOUR: SACRED GEOGRAPHY

For information concerning the Sacred Headwaters and the efforts of the Tahltan to protect their homeland in the Stikine, visit the following websites: www.skeenawatershed.com and www.sacredheadwaters.com. I spent a year in a logging camp on Haida Gwaii and wrote of the experience in the essay "In the Shadow of Red Cedar," published in *The Clouded Leopard* (Vancouver: Douglas & McIntyre, 1998).

For two fine books on the cultural importance of coca see C. J. Allen, *The Hold Life Has: Coca and Cultural Identity in an Andean Community* (Washington, D.C.: Smithsonian Institution Press, 1988), and Anthony Henman, *Mama Coca* (London: Hassle Free Press, 1978).

There is a vast literature on the Inca and contemporary Andean ethnography. For history of the Inca, see Louis Baudin, *Daily Life in Peru Under the Last Incas* (New York: Macmillan, 1968); Brian Bauer's *The Development of the Inca State* (Austin: University of Texas Press, 1992) and *Ancient Cuzco: Heartland of the Inca* (Austin: University of Texas Press, 2004); B. C. Brundage, *Lords of Cuzco* (1967) and *Empire of the Inca* (1963), both reprinted (Norman: University of Oklahoma Press, 1985); R. Burger, C. Morris, and R. Matos Mendieta, eds., *Variations in the Expression of Inka Power: A Symposium at Dumbarton Oaks, 18 and 19 October 1997* (Washington, D.C.: Dumbarton Oaks Research Library and Collection, 2007); G. W. Conrad and A. Demarest, *Religion and Empire* (Cambridge: Cambridge University Press, 1984); T. D'Altroy, *The Incas* (Oxford: Blackwell, 2002); J. Hemming, *The Conquest of the Incas* (New York: Harcourt Brace Jovanovich, 1970); C. Morris and A. von Hagen, *The Inka Empire and its Andean Origins* (New York: Abbeville Press, 1993); M. Moseley, *The Incas and their Ancestors: The Archaeology of Peru* (London: Thames & Hudson, 1992); K. MacQuarrie, *The Last Days of the Incas* (New York: Simon & Schuster, 2007); A. Métraux, *The History of the Incas* (New York: Schocken Books, 1979); J. H. Rowe, "Inca Culture at the Time of the Spanish Conquest," in J. H. Steward, ed., *Handbook of South American Indians*, Bureau of American Ethnology Bulletin 143, vol. 2 (Washington, D.C.: U.S. Government Printing Office, 1946), 183–330; and R. T. Zuidema, *Inca Civilization in Cuzco* (Austin: University of Texas Press, 1990).

For reprints of early accounts from the Chronicles, see: J. de Acosta, *Natural and Moral History of the Indies*, ed. Jane Mangan (Durham, N.C.: Duke University Press, 2002); J. de Betanzos, *Narrative of the Incas*, trans. and ed. Roland Hamilton and Dana Buchanan (Austin:

University of Texas Press, 1996); B. Cobo, *Inca Religion and Customs* (1653), trans. and ed. Roland Hamilton (Austin: University of Texas Press, 1990); B. Cobo, *History of the Inca Empire* (1653), trans. and ed. Roland Hamilton (Austin: University of Texas Press, 1983); Garcilaso de la Vega, *The Royal Commentaries of the Incas and General History of Peru, Parts 1 & 2* (1609), trans. Harold Livermore (Austin: University of Texas Press, 1966); Poma Huamán Poma de Ayaala, *Letter to a King*, ed. Christopher Dilke (New York: Dutton, 1978); Pedro Sarmiento de Gamboa, *The History of the Incas* (1572), trans. and ed. Brian Bauer and Vania Smith (Austin: University of Texas Press, 2007); Pedro de Cieza de León, *The Incas*, (1554), ed. Victor W. von Hagen (Norman: University of Oklahoma Press, 1976).

For Andean notions of land, pilgrimage, and sacred geography, see: M. J. Sallnow, *Pilgrims of the Andes* (Washington, D.C.: Smithsonian Institution Press, 1987); B. Bauer and C. Stanish, *Ritual and Pilgrimage in the Ancient Andes: The Islands of the Sun and the Moon* (Austin: University of Texas Press, 2001); B. Bauer, *The Sacred Landscape of the Inca: The Cusco Ceque System* (Austin: University of Texas Press, 1998); and R. T. Zuidema, *The Ceque System of Cuzco: The Social Organization of the Capital of the Inca* (Leiden: E. J. Brill, 1964). Johan Reinhard has written several important books, including *The Ice Maiden: Inca Mummies, Mountain Gods, and Sacred Sites in the Andes* (Washington, D.C.: National Geographic Society, 2005) and *Machu Picchu: Exploring an Ancient Sacred Center*, 4th rev. ed. (Los Angeles: Cotsen Institute of Archaeology, UCLA, 2007). For an excellent study of the Qoyllur Rit'I, see: Robert Randall, "Qoyllur Rit'I, An Inca Festival of the Pleides," *Boletin del Instituto Frances de Estudios Andinos* 11, (1-2):37-81 (Lima).

For astronomy, see: Brian Bauer and David Dearborn, *Astronomy and Empire in the Ancient Andes* (Austin: University of Texas Press, 1995); G. Urton, *At the Crossroads of the Earth and the Sky: An Andean Cosmology* (Austin: University of Texas Press, 1981). For Inca roads see: J. Hyslop, *The Inka Road System* (New York: Academic Press, 1984), and Victor W. von Hagen, *Highway of the Sun* (Boston: Little, Brown, 1955). See also J. Hyslop, *Inka Settlement Planning* (Austin:

University of Texas Press, 1990). For excellent books on the Andean Khipu system of accounting, see: G. Urton, *Signs of the Inka Khipu: Binary Coding in the Andean Knotted String Records* (Austin: University of Texas Press, 2003), and J. Quilter and G. Urton, eds., *Narrative Threads: Accounting and Recounting in Andean Khipu* (Austin: University of Texas Press, 2002).

For classic ethnographies see: T. A. Abercrombie, *Pathways of Memory and Power: Ethnography and History Among an Andean People* (Madison: University of Wisconsin Press, 1998); J. W. Bastien, *Mountain of the Condor: Metaphor and Ritual in an Andean Ayllu* (Long Grove, Ill.: Waveland Press, 1985); Inge Bolin's *Growing Up in a Culture of Respect: Child Rearing in Highland Peru* (Austin: University of Texas Press, 2006) and *Rituals of Respect: The Secret of Survival in the High Peruvian Andes* (Austin: University of Texas Press, 1998); S. Brush, *Mountain, Field, and Family: The Economy and Human Ecology of an Andean Valley* (Philadelphia: University of Pennsylvania Press, 1977); J. Meyerson, *'Tambo: Life in an Andean Village* (Austin: University of Texas Press, 1990); B. J. Isbell, *To Defend Ourselves: Ecology and Ritual in an Andean Village* (Austin: University of Texas Press, 1978); and F. Salomon, *The Cord Keepers: Khipus and Cultural Life in a Peruvian Village* (Durham, N.C.: Duke University Press, 2004). For the history of the Vilcabamba, last redoubt of the Inca, see: H. Thomson, *The White Rock: An Exploration of the Inca Heartland* (Woodstock, N.Y.: Overlook Press, 2003), and V. Lee, *Forgotten Vilcabamba: Final Stronghold of the Incas* (Jackson Hole, Wyo.: Empire Publishing, 2000).

For Andean textile traditions, see: Nilda Callañaupa Alvarez, *Weaving in the Peruvian Highlands: Dreaming Patterns, Weaving Memories* (Loveland, Col.: Interweave Press, 2007). For Andean ethnobotany see: J. Bastien, *Healers of the Andes: Kallawaya Herbalists and Their Medicinal Plants* (Salt Lake City: University of Utah Press, 1987); C. Franquemont, T. Plowman, E. Franquemont, et al., *The Ethnobotany of Chinchero, an Andean Community in Southern Peru*, Fieldiana, Botany New Series No. 24 (Chicago: Field Museum of Natural History, 1990).

For a wonderful portrait of contemporary Peru, see Ron Wright, *Cut Stones and Crossroads* (New York: Penguin Books, 1984). For a terrific and very funny travel account covering the Sierra Nevada de Santa Marta before the rise of the drug trade, see: Charles Nicholl, *The Fruit Palace* (London: Heinemann, 1985).

For insight into the world of the Elder Brothers, the late Gerardo Reichel-Dolmatoff is again a fundamental source. His monograph, published in two volumes in 1950 and 1951, was reprinted in 1985; see *Los Kogi: Una Tribu de la Sierra Nevada de Santa Marta, Colombia*, 2 vols. (Bogotá: Nueva Biblioteca Colombiana de Procultura, Editorial Presencia, 1985). In addition, see the following writings by Reichel-Dolmatoff: *The Sacred Mountain of Colombia's Kogi Indians* (Leiden: E. J. Brill, 1990); "Training for the Priesthood Among the Kogi of Colombia" in J. Wilbert, ed., *Enculturation in Latin America: An Anthology* (Los Angeles: UCLA Latin American Center Publications, 1976); "The Loom of Life: A Kogi Principle of Integration," *Journal of Latin American Lore* 4, no. 1 (1978): 5–27; "The Great Mother and the Kogi Universe: A Concise Overview," *Journal of Latin American Lore* 13, no. 1 (1987): 73–113; "Templos Kogi: Introducción al Simbolismo y a la Astronomía del Espacio Sacrado," *Revista Colombiana de Antropología* 19 (1975): 199–246; and *Indians of Colombia: Experience and Cognition* (Bogotá: Villegas Editores, 1991). For Arhuaco mythology and ritual, see: Donald Tayler, *The Coming of the Sun*, Pitt Rivers Museum Monograph No. 7 (Oxford: University of Oxford, 1997). See also: Alan Ereira, *The Elder Brothers' Warning* (London: Tairona Heritage Trust, 2009). In 1991, Alan Ereira and Graham Townsley made *From the Heart of the World*, a powerful film that brought the message of the Kogi and the Elder Brothers to the world. Ereira later established the Tairona Heritage Trust (www.tairona.myzen.co.uk), a non-profit organization that works closely with Gonawindua (www.tairona.org), the official organization of the indigenous peoples of the Sierra Nevada de Santa Marta.

For an understanding of the Dreaming and the Songlines, I do not find Bruce Chatwin's popular book, *The Songlines* (New York: Penguin, 1988), very helpful. The most provocative and elegant exploration of the subtle philosophy of the Aboriginal civilization is W. E. H. Stanner's "The Dreaming," in his collection *White Man Got No Dreaming: Essays, 1938–1973* (Canberra: Australian National University Press, 1979). For other classic accounts, see: Ronald Berndt and Catherine Berndt, *The Speaking Land* (Sydney: Penguin Books, 1988), and *The World of the First Australians* (Canberra: Aboriginal Studies Press, 1988); A. P. Elkin, *The Australian Aborigines*, 4th ed. (Sydney: Angus and Robertson, 1976); and T. G. H. Strehlow's *Aranda Traditions* (Melbourne: Melbourne University Press, 1974) and *Songs of Central Australia* (Sydney: Angus and Robertson, 1971). See also: John Mulvaney and Johan Kamminga, *Prehistory of Australia* (St. Leonards, Australia: Allen & Unwin, 1999); Richard Baker, *Land Is Life: From Bush to Town: The Story of the Yanyuwa People* (St. Leonards, Australia: Allen & Unwin, 1999); Fred Myers, *Pintupi Country, Pintupi Self: Sentiment, Place, and Politics among Western Desert Aborigines* (Berkeley: University of California Press, 1991); Robert Tonkinson and Michael Howard, eds., *Going It Alone?: Prospects for Aboriginal Autonomy* (Canberra: Aboriginal Studies Press, 1990); and Robert Tonkinson's *The Mardu Aborigines: Living the Dream in Australia's Desert* (Fort Worth, Tex.: Holt, Rinehart and Winston, 1991) and *The Jigalong Mob: Aboriginal Victors of the Desert Crusade* (Menlo Park, Calif.: Benjamin Cummings Publishing Co., 1974).

For the clash of cultures and the consequences see: Bruce Elder, *Blood on the Wattle: Massacres and Maltreatment of Aboriginal Australians Since 1788* (Sydney: New Holland, 2002); Alistair Paterson, *The Lost Legions: Culture Contact in Colonial Australia* (Plymouth, England: Altamira Press, 2008). For the wonder of Aboriginal art, see: Fred Myers, *Painting Culture: The Making of a High Aboriginal Art* (Durham, N.C.: Duke University Press, 2002). For a popular survey and introduction see: Robert Lawlor, *Voices of the First Day: Awakening in the Aboriginal Dreamtime* (Rochester, Vt.: Inner Traditions, 1991).

CHAPTER FIVE: CENTURY OF THE WIND

The title of this chapter comes from the third volume of Eduardo Galeano's astonishing trilogy, *Memory of Fire* (New York: Pantheon Books, 1985, 1987, 1988). For the Garden of Eden see Nicholas Wade, "Eden? Maybe. But Where's the Apple Tree?" *New York Times* (April 30, 2009). See also: Sarah Tishkoff et al., "The Genetic Structure and History of Africans and African Americans," *Science* 324, no. 5930 (May 2009): 1035–44. For Mazatec whistle speech, see: G. M. Cowan, "Mazateco Whistle Speech," *Language* 24, no. 3 (1948): 280–86. For a sense of the mystical realm of Vodoun, please see my two books on Haiti: *The Serpent and the Rainbow* (New York: Simon & Schuster, 1985) and *Passage of Darkness* (Chapel Hill: University of North Carolina Press, 1988). For the Naxi see: Cai Hua, *A Society Without Fathers or Husbands: The Na of China* (Brooklyn: Zone Books, 2008). For the Warao, see: Johannes Wilbert's, *Mindful of Famine: Religious Climatology of the Warao Indians* (Cambridge, Mass.: Harvard University Press, 1996); *Mystic Endowment: Religious Ethnography of the Warao Indians* (Cambridge: Harvard University Press, 1993); and *Tobacco and Shamanism in South America* (New Haven, Ct.: Yale University Press, 1993). For the Mentawai aesthetic, see: Charles Lindsay, *Mentawai Shaman: Keeper of the Rain Forest* (New York: Aperture, 1992).

For the Tendai marathon monks and the traditions of the Yamabushi, see: Carmen Blacker, *The Catalpa Bow: A Study of Shamanistic Practices in Japan* (London: Allen & Unwin, 1975); Miyake Hitoshi, *Shugendō: Essays on the Structure of Japanese Folk Religion* (Ann Arbor, Mich.: Center for Japanese Studies, University of Michigan, 2001); Miyake Hitoshi, *The Mandala of the Mountain: Shugendō and Folk Religion*, ed. Gaynor Sekimori (Tokyo: Keio University Press, 2005); Paul Swanson, ed., *Tendai Buddhism in Japan, Japanese Journal of Religious Studies* 14, nos. 2–3 (1987); Royall Tyler and Paul Swanson, eds., *Shugendo and Mountain Religion in Japan, Japanese Journal of Religious Studies* 16, nos. 2–3 (1989); Percival Lowell, *Occult Japan* (Boston: Houghton Mifflin, 1895); and John Stevens, *The Marathon Monks of Mount Hiei* (Boston: Shambhala, 1988).

To understand all of these complex notions of culture, the finest source, the ultimate voice, is the late David Maybury-Lewis, who taught me almost everything I know about anthropology. Please see his classic publications: *Akwe-Shavante Society* (Oxford: Clarendon Press, 1967); *Dialectical Societies* (Cambridge, Mass.: Harvard University Press, 1979); *Indigenous Peoples, Ethnic Groups, and the State* (1965; reprint, Boston: Allyn and Bacon, 1997); *The Savage and the Innocent* (Boston: Beacon Press, 2000); his edited work, *The Politics of Ethnicity: Indigenous Peoples in Latin American States* (Cambridge, Mass.: Harvard University Press, 2002); and *Millennium: Tribal Wisdom and the Modern World* (New York: Viking, 1992).

For the Kiowa see: J. Mooney, "Calendar History of the Kiowa, Indians," *Seventeenth Annual Report of the Bureau of American Ethnology* (Washington, D.C.: Smithsonian Institution Press, 1898), 129–445; *One River* (New York: Simon & Schuster, 1996); Weston LaBarre, *The Peyote Cult* (1938), 5th ed., enl. (Norman: University of Oklahoma Press, 1989). For the systematic elimination of the buffalo, see: Andrew Isenberg, *The Destruction of the Bison: An Environmental History, 1750–1920* (Cambridge: Cambridge University Press, 2000). For the horrors of the rubber era in the Putumayo, see: Norman Thomson, *The Putumayo Red Book* (London: N. Thomson & Co., 1913); R. Collier, *The River that God Forgot* (London: Collins, 1968); W. E. Hardenburg, *The Putumayo: The Devil's Paradise* (London: T. Fisher Unwin, 1912); B. Weinstein, *The Amazon Rubber Boom, 1850–1920* (Stanford, Calif.: Stanford University Press, 1983).

For the voices of the Penan and the quotes from various Malaysian officials, see: Wade Davis, Ian MacKenzie, and Shane Kennedy, *Nomads of the Dawn: The Penan of the Borneo Rain Forest* (San Francisco: Pomegranate Press, 1995). To support Bruno Manser's legacy, please contact Bruno Manser Fonds, www.bmf.ch/en/. See also: "Dreams of a Jade Forest," a profile I wrote of Bruno, later published in *The Clouded Leopard* (Vancouver: Douglas & McIntyre, 1998), 57–72.

For Pol Pot and the Killing Fields see: David Chandler, *Brother Number One: A Political Biography of Pol Pot* (Boulder, Col.: Westview Press, 1999); Dith Pran, *Children of Cambodia's Killing Fields: Memoirs by Survivors* (Chiang Mai, Thailand: Silkworm Books, 1997); Ben Kiernan's *How Pol Pot Came to Power: Colonialism, Nationalism, and Communism in Cambodia, 1930–1975* (New Haven, Ct.: Yale University Press, 2004), and *The Pol Pot Regime: Race, Power, and Genocide in Cambodia under the Khmer Rouge, 1975–79* (New Haven, Ct.: Yale University Press, 2008); and Loung Ung, *First They Killed My Father: A Daughter of Cambodia Remembers* (New York: Perennial, 2000).

The best single history of Tibet since the Chinese revolution is: Tsering Shakya, *The Dragon in the Land of the Snows: A History of Modern Tibet since 1947* (New York: Columbia University Press, 1999). See also: M. C. Goldstein, *A History of Modern Tibet, 1913–1951* (Berkeley: University of California Press, 1989), and Tubten Khetsun, *Memories of Life in Lhasa Under Chinese Rule* (New York: Columbia University Press, 2008). Two fine popular histories are: Charles Allen, *The Search for Shangri-La: A Journey into Tibetan History* (London: Little, Brown, 1999), and Patrick French, *Tibet, Tibet: A Personal History of a Lost Land* (London: HarperCollins, 2003).

Matthieu Ricard and his father, philosopher Jean-François Revel, spent a week in conversation at a teahouse in Katmandu. Their unedited discussions are one of the best introductions to the Tibetan dharma path. See: Jean-François Revel and Matthieu Ricard, *The Monk and the Philosopher: East Meets West in a Father–Son Dialogue* (London: Thorsons, 1999). See also: Matthieu Ricard and Trinh Xuan Thuan, *The Quantum and the Lotus: A Journey to the Frontiers Where Science and Buddhism Meet* (New York: Three Rivers Press, 1999), as well as the following works by Matthieu Ricard: *Happiness: A Guide to Developing Life's Most Important Skill* (New York: Little, Brown, 2007); *Motionless Journey: From a Hermitage in the Himalayas* (London: Thames & Hudson, 2008); *Tibet: An Inner Journey* (London: Thames & Hudson, 2007); *Journey to Enlightenment: The Life and World of Khyentse Rinpoche, Spiritual Teacher from Tibet* (New York: Aperture, 1996); and *Bhutan: The Land of Serenity* (London: Thames & Hudson, 2009).

For the plight of the pastoral nomads of northern Kenya, see: Elliot Fratkin and Eric Abella Roth, eds., *As Pastoralists Settle: Social, Health, and Economic Consequences of the Pastoral Sedentarization in Marsabit District, Kenya* (New York: Springer, 2005); Carolyn Lesorogol, *Contesting the Commons: Privatizing Pastoral Lands in Kenya* (Ann Arbor: University of Michigan Press, 2008). For a beautiful and informative illustrated book, see: Nigel Pavitt, *Samburu* (New York: Henry Holt, 1991). See also my discussion in *Light at the Edge of the World* (Vancouver: Douglas & McIntyre, 2007).

For a brilliant perspective on the consequences of the breakdown of culture, see: Robert Kaplan's *The Ends of the Earth: From Togo to Turkmenistan, from Iran to Cambodia, a Journey to the Frontiers of Anarchy* (New York: Vintage, 1997), and *The Coming Anarchy: Shattering the Dreams of the Post Cold War* (New York: Vintage, 2001). See also: John Bodley's *Victims of Progress*, 5th ed. (Lanham, Md.: Altamira Press, 2008), and *Anthropology and Contemporary Human Problems*, 5th ed. (Lanham, Md.: Altamira Press, 2008). For the atrocities in the Democratic Republic of Congo see: Bob Herbert, "The Invisible War," *New York Times* (February 21, 2009), A17.

There is, of course, a vast literature on the Arctic, but were I to suggest three books they would be: Pierre Berton, *Arctic Grail: The Quest for the Northwest Passage and the North Pole, 1818–1909* (Guilford, Conn.: Lyons Press, 2000); Hugh Brody, *Living Arctic: Hunters of the Canadian North* (Seattle: University of Washington Press, 1990); and Gretel Erhlich, *This Cold Heaven: Seven Seasons in Greenland* (New York: Vintage Books, 2003). For Peter Freuchen, see his *Arctic Adventure: My Life in the Frozen North* (Guilford, Conn.: Lyons Press, 2002), and *Book of the Eskimos* (London: Bramhall House, 1961). See also my essay "Hunters of the Northern Ice," in *The Clouded Leopard* (Vancouver: Douglas & McIntyre, 1998), 31–55.

For two superb books on the consequences of climate change, especially in regard to glacial recession, see: Ben Orlove, Ellen Wiegandt, and Brian Luckman, eds., *Darkening Peaks: Glacial Retreat, Science, and Society* (Berkeley: University of California Press, 2008), and Gary Braasch, *Earth Under Fire: How Global Warming Is Changing the World* (Berkeley: University of California Press, 2007). See also: Thom Hartmann, *The Last Hours of Ancient Sunlight* (New York: Three Rivers Press, 2004). On the plight of the River Ganges, see: Emily Wax, "A Sacred River Endangered by Global Warming," *Washington Post* (June 17, 2007), A14. For the loss of the stalagmite in Amarnath Cave, see: "Holy Stalagmite Can't Take the Heat," a Guardian News Service report, *Globe and Mail* (July 3, 2007), L5. For the insect infestations in the North American West, see: Jim Robbins, "Spread of Bark Beetle Kills Millions of Acres of Trees in West," *New York Times* (November 18, 2008), D3.

For splendid accounts of the Sahara, and of Timbuktu and the salt caravans to Taoudenni, see: Michael Benanav, *Men of Salt: Across the Sahara with the Caravan of White Gold* (Guilford, Conn.: Lyons Press, 2008); Mark Kurlansky, *Salt: A World History* (New York: Walker and Co., 2002); Marq de Villiers and Sheila Hirtle, *Sahara: A Natural History* (New York: Walker and Co., 2002); Mark Jenkins, *To Timbuktu: A Journey Down the Niger* (New York: Quill, 1998); William Langewiesche, *Sahara Unveiled: A Journey Across the Desert* (New York: Vintage Books, 1996).

For a final vision of hope, see the works of Father Thomas Berry, especially *The Dream of the Earth* (San Francisco: Sierra Club Books, 1988); *Evening Thoughts: Reflecting on Earth as Sacred Community* (San Francisco: Sierra Club Books, 2006); and *The Great Work: Our Way Into the Future* (New York: Three Rivers Press, 1999).

ACKNOWLEDGEMENTS

I would like to acknowledge with gratitude the many friends and colleagues who contributed to the expeditions that in good measure inspired these lectures. At the National Geographic Society (NGS) I would like to thank Terry Garcia and his team at Mission Programs, Susan Reeve, Jim Bullard, Lynn Cutter, Greg McGruder, Deborah Benson, Mark Bauman as well as Oliver Payne, Tim Kelly, Chris Leidel, Terry Adamson, John Fahey, John Rasmus, Keith Bellows and Spencer Wells. The film series *Light at the Edge of the World* originated at National Geographic Channel (Canada) and 90th Parallel Productions in Toronto, in partnership with the National Geographic Channel (International). Thanks to Gordon Henderson, Cindy Witten, Stephen Hunter, Martha Conboy, and especially to Sydney Suissa and Andrew Gregg, who directed all four films. Andy and I had worked together on an episode for the CBC biography strand *Life and Times*. The idea of doing a longer series based on my book *Light at the Edge of the World* emerged out of that project, and it made for a wonderful collaboration. For their terrific work in the field and studio my thanks go to Rick Boston, Wade Carson, Paul Freer, Mike Josselyn, Geoff Matheson, Sanjay Mehta and John Tran.

Thanks in Nepal to Tsetsam Ani, Sherab Barma, Thomas Kelly, Matthieu Ricard, Trulshik Rinpoche, and particularly to Carroll Dunham. In the Arctic thanks are due to the people of Igloolik and Qaanaaq, and especially to John Arnatsiaq, Jens Danielsen, Graham Dickson, Gretel Ehrlich, Theo Ikummaq, Olayuk and Martha Narqitarvik. Lori Dynan at the NGS introduced me to Nainoa Thompson and the Polynesian Voyaging Society. Special thanks to Lori and to Nainoa as well as Ka'iulani Murphy, Tava Taupu, Jeffrey Omai and Mau Piailug. For guidance and insight on Rapa Nui I am indebted to my friends Claudio Cristino, Alexandra Edwards, Edmundo Edwards and Patricia Vargas. In Peru, Johan Reinhard and Nilda Callañaupa shared their unique experiences and knowledge. I have known both for many years, and as always they were a delight to be with.

For their support for the second series of films, another four hours that were produced by National Geographic Television for the National Geographic Channel, I would like to thank Stephen Hunter and Sydney Suissa, as well as Marie Wiljanen, Victoria Kirker, Cherry Yates, Korin Anderson, Tobias Louie, Nicole Teusch, Carrie Regan, and especially John Mernit and his entire team at NG Television. It was a privilege to work with three inspired directors, Graham Townsley in the Sierra Nevada, David Shadrack Smith and his colleagues at Part2Pictures in Australia, and Howard Reid in both Mongolia and the Northwest Amazon of Colombia. Thanks as well to Jim Cricchi, Cindy D'Agostino, Robert Neufeld, Emmanuel Mairesse and Dan Marks.

In Japan, my thanks go to Gaynor Sekimori, who opened the doors to the Tendai monks and the rich traditions of Shugendo. Werner Wilbert introduced me to the Winikina Warao in the Orinoco delta. With Peter von Puttkamer I travelled to the Mazatec in Oaxaca, the Navaho in New Mexico, and the Cofán in Ecuador where Randy Borman received us very kindly. Charles Lindsay introduced me to the Mentawai of Siberut. In Mongolia I had the good fortune to work with Dalanbayor, Jendupdorj, Mukhdalai and family, Lama Pasang Suren, Lama Lusang Ravjam, Namjin and family, Thomas Kelly, Carroll Dunham, Alfonse Roy, Nandu Kumar, and Bat Amgalan Lhagvajav.

In the Sierra Nevada de Santa Marta of Colombia, thanks are due to Jaime Andres Cujaban, Ramon Gill, Roberto Mojica, Peter Diaz Porta, Alfonse Roy, Eugenio Villafaña, Danilo Villafaña and Rogelio Mejia as well as to the many indigenous organizations who formally welcomed our collaboration: Bunkwanarrua Tayrona, Organización Gonavindua Tayrona, Organización Wiwa Yugumaian, Organización Indígena Kankwama, Confederación Indígena Tayrona.

In Australia, Carrie Williamson introduced us to Adam McFie, a brilliant anthropologist, who in turn brought us into the world of Otto Bulmaniya Campion and his wife Christine and their wonderful family, as well as Peter Djigirr, Peter Girrikirri, Richard Bandalil. Thanks too to the Ramingining Rangers, Lindsay Wile, Jeremy Ashton, Ray Whear and the Jawoyn Association and to anthropologist Bob Tonkinson for his advice and guidance.

Time among the Barasana and their neighbours was facilitated by Ambassador of Colombia to the United States Carolina Barco and her colleagues Denisse Yanovich, Mercede Hannabergh de Uribe and General Edgar Ceballos. The collaboration with Asociación de Capitanes Indígenas de Piráparaná (ACAIPI) and the peoples of the Pirapará was made possible by my good friend Martin von Hildebrand and his colleagues at Fundación Gaia Amazonas, including Nelson Ortiz, Silvia Gomez, Natalia Hernández and Jorge Kahi. In the field we were joined by anthropologist Stephen Hugh-Jones, who shared his profound knowledge, acquired over a lifetime of intense dedication to place, with an immense generosity of spirit. We were guided along the way by Barasana and Makuna scholars of extraordinary depth, insight and sensitivity: Maximiliano García, Roberto Marín, Ricardo Marín, Rosa Marín, Reinel Ortega. Our crew, Ryan Hill, Peter Diaz Porta, Yesid Ricardo Vasquez and Diana Rico, were joyous, a delight to work with. Thanks as well to ACAIPI and to all the communities and peoples of the river.

The journey into the Sahara, described briefly at the end of these lectures, was made possible by Roberto Cerea and his remarkable team at TransAfrica. Joining us on that adventure and sharing their wisdom were Alex and Caroline Chadwick, Isa Mohamed, Baba Omar and Professor Salem Ould. In East Africa I was guided by Kevin Smith and Jonathan Lengalen. My thanks in Sarawak to all the Penan people and their supporters, most notably Lejeng Kusin, Anderson Mutang Urud, Asik Nyelit, Tu'o Pejuman and Mutang Tu'o, Ian MacKenzie, Bruno Manser and Peter Brosius.

For everything else, all of these friendships that made these adventures possible, the many people who provided a home, a point of return, I would like to acknowledge Darlene and Jeff Anderson, Monty and Pashan Bassett, Tom Buri, Natalie Charlton, Lavinia Currier, Simon and Cindy Davies, Oscar Dennis, Lindsay and Patti Eberts, Clayton and Caryl Eshleman, Stephen Ferry, Guujaaw, Peter Jakesta, Sven Lindblad, Barbara and Greg MacGillivray, Peter Matson, David Maybury-Lewis, Frederico Medem, Richard Nault, Richard Overstall, Tim Plowman, Travis Price, Rhoda Quock, Tom Rafael, Chris Rainier, Gerardo Reichel-Dolmatoff, Richard Evans Schultes, Dan Taylor, Kevin Smith, Peter and Sheera von Puttkamer, Tim Ward, and Leo and Angie Wells.

At the CBC my thanks go to Philip Coulter and Bernie Lucht. At House of Anansi Press I would like to thank Lynn Henry, a wonderful editor, as well as Sarah MacLachlan, Laura Repas, Janie Yoon, and Bill Douglas for his cover design.

As always, the final word of thanks goes to my sister Karen and my loving family, Gail, Tara and Raina.

INDEX